CW01496829

# The Joy of Knowing Fuck All

## *What Awaits Beyond Ideas of Truth*

## Phil Goddard

**The Joy of Knowing Fuck All**

Published by The Happy Discovery - www.thehappydiscovery.com

Cover Design: Emily Nature

Contact the author:  www.philg.com

First Edition.

ISBN: 9798612556060

D: 20200229

For Believers Everywhere

# CONTENTS

*"There isn't time, so brief is life, for bickerings, apologies, heartburnings, callings to account. There is only time for loving, and but an instant, so to speak, for that."*

*~Mark Twain*

At first I had no idea what I was doing, and strived to know. Then I realised I didn't need to know what I was doing. Then I realised it wasn't even me doing it...

# Hello...

When I told a friend it felt a bit of a cheat releasing another book containing articles I've posted on social media, his tongue-in-cheek reply had me laugh out loud:

*"Yeah you're right, writing a book is supposed to be hard work and labour intensive. Not just fun and random stuff that comes to you in the moment."*

My first two books, *Musings on Love* and *More Musings on Love,* came about in the same way. They have been enjoyed by many readers, some of whom have become clients who have experienced beautiful changes in their lives.

This third book is a similar format, short chapters that can be read and reflected upon, each pointing to peace, love and freedom.

But this book was written entirely after seeing something new during a conversation in late 2017. Up until then I had spent 19 years exploring many spiritual understandings, including the Three Principles and Non-Duality, and studied a whole bunch of other stuff. That insight revealed to me something about all of it, something that initially was disorientating, to the extent that I 'hid in a cave' for a while until the mushroom cloud settled.

A new clarity appeared, and there's now a peace and freedom that has arisen, or rather that has been allowed. It has come from seeing anew the nature of beliefs, the nature of truth, ideas and concepts, and how our attachment to them shapes our experience of life.

It is often our searching and subsequent attachment to an understanding or paradigm that keeps us from freedom and peace in our quest to know, believe and understand.

It has also helped me see how our belief in knowing, our belief in truth, so often leads to disconnection and separation, even in communities teaching non-separation.

This is a book of ideas, a point to note: Nothing in this book is true. It contains ideas about ideas, because really that's all we've got. Ideas about ideas, beliefs and truth, and of course, ideas about Love.

It is a book about freedom from knowing, the freedom of seeing the nature of beliefs, ideas and concepts, and the joy that is available to us, always, irrespective of our searching and quest to understand and know.

It is about the freedom of seeing the nature of knowing and the joy of realising we know nothing, no thing.

The joy of knowing f*#k all.

**A word on True Essence and Love:**

A few times in this book I have referred to your 'true essence' and occasionally mention your 'true self.' I have more recently refrained from using these terms because they are so easily misunderstood to mean yet another concept, another 'thing' for us to search out and find.

Spiritual teachers have for millennia attempted to describe what this 'true essence' actually is, and I will not attempt to do so in the introduction of a book. It is not possible to describe using language since the moment we use words we enter into metaphor and can only describe a concept.

Suffice to say that where I have used these terms I am pointing to what it is to be human, whatever that is, without any concepts or ideas. Paradoxically, even without the concept of true nature, something I explicitly point out later in the book. The you without any ideas of you. The you without any ideas at all, even ideas of God.

In the aftermath of that insight I also started to see Love differently. Once again, not something I can summarise in this introduction, but a few words spoken to me by a coach helped me see how much of my understanding of Love was based on ideas and concepts. Actually all of it!

In some of the chapters in this book I refer to our true essence as Love.

Ask me today and I'll tell you Love is my favourite idea. Whether we can really know our true essence or know Love is a debate similar in magnitude to whether we can know God, and nations have fought over this for generations.

Perhaps rather than our perpetual search to know, there is freedom in giving up the search and simply allowing life to show us.

But of course for us to be shown we must be willing to see, and to really see we surely must first start with eyes that are unfiltered and not contaminated by all our conditioned beliefs, ideas and concepts.

Or at least understand that is what is going on, that there will always be beliefs, ideas and concepts and that even when we think we know, we really know fuck all.

And we can surely revel in the joy of that!

*The world looks the way it does because you're looking at it that way.*

# Stop the Search!

*'You think it works like that, but it doesn't, it works like this, how I see it, which is how you would see if only you looked in the direction I suggest. And when you look in that direction I'll help you add meaning and interpret what you see. Meantime, you're wrong and it's understandable, but the only way to peace is to see it the same as me.'* ~Profound Spiritual Teacher

Does this look familiar? This kind of message is ubiquitous, and certainly prevalent on social media. I've even written similar myself and included a bunch of stuff like this in my first couple of books, both written before an insight I had in 2017.

Show me pretty much any writing, any social media post, any teachings, and I'll show you a belief, even when and especially where the teacher is presenting a truth. If you look closely, you'll see even the teachers themselves being hoodwinked by beliefs, some making claims that they are not interpreting, yet in the same message suggesting someone meant something different to the words that were used.

Then there's the 'I switched from belief to truth' story. It goes something like this:

'I spent years looking at x, believing it to be true, yet was still confused/unhappy and something felt amiss. Then I stumbled upon y, which I could see is true, and the confusion/unhappiness dissolved/became irrelevant.'

Basically, there was a switch from believing one thing that didn't quite make sense or bring peace to believing something else, that appears to make sense and either brought some peace, or explain in a much more believable way what is actually going on.

'Aha! Now I really understand why I'm suffering and actually how it's not the real me that suffers.'

Spoiler alert: it's your interpretation and subsequent belief that has satisfied your desire to understand, which has in turn had you stop searching and therefore feel at peace.

I used to believe only love was true and love was all there is. (More on this later…)

*"But wait! If you inquire into experience that is what you'll see!"*

Ah yes, we're sometimes encouraged to inquire into experience, which is what had people believe the world is flat. Experience tells us nothing without interpretation. Interpretation is always a process of meaning creation.

You'll often see layers upon layers of logical argument built upon a premise that is presented as truth, and in such communities many of these layers become new truths upon which other teachings are based, calling out others who use the same words in different ways as wrong.

It can, of course, all be good fun. But certainly not always, discussions often laced with accusations of bullying, taking swipes, making the impersonal personal, and much arguing over 'truths'...

All these debates are dependent upon one thing - belief. Even and especially the claims of truth. They are dependent upon belief because they have to be.

For something to make sense to us we have to interpret it, and we have to believe that interpretation.

If it makes sense, you're believing something.

We're obsessed with interpretation and understanding, because the seeker in us all wants to make sense of life. Especially when it presents to us a hook for us to moor our boat in which we've sailed through years of searching.

You might see it - 'when you discover who you truly are the search is over.' You might even see claims of knowing who or what God is, what God or Consciousness does. Like we can know...

Here's a tip: If someone suggests they know who or what God is check their pulse. If they have one they're lying.

I suggest something else. When you discover the nature of searching, the nature of seeing, the nature of beliefs and the nature of truth, you may come to realise the fallacy of searching, and indeed still search anyways. You'll likely see searching, beliefs and truth in a different light.

Almost all coaches and spiritual teachers help you to see 'something', generally a new concept or idea labelled as truth. A new paradigm, a bit like offering you alternative coloured sunglasses - "Here, try these, they are clear."

In the last couple of years I've focused much more on helping people understand the nature of seeing and the nature of truth, like helping you understand you're always wearing sunglasses, even when you believe you're not.

In understanding the nature of beliefs, the nature of seeing and the nature of truth, there seems to be little point in criticising others for what they see and for how they interpret what they see. Because we're ALL doing it. Or, as the non-dualists might say, 'it's being done.'

Millennia of wars over what beliefs are true, debates over who is right and who is wrong, discussions of differences as part of the quest to help us understand we're all the same and all of the same. The quest for it to make sense.

This book aims to show you it doesn't need to make sense and that peace is always available.

Irrespective of what you believe you know.

# Love is the Point of Everything

Imagine the scenario... you're at home, sitting on your sofa with your family, maybe playing a game together, watching a movie together, or just chatting, giggling, being...

Then someone calls at your door. You reluctantly get up to answer, and it's some pumped up Tony Robbins style guy, who talks to you in that deep, gruff voice, pointing a finger at you.

'You could have an AMAZING life, achieve AMAZING things, experience extraordinary, profoundly fulfilling, tangible results, if you hired someone like me!' he exclaims energetically. "Don't waste your life, live your life, take massive action, seek constant and never-ending improvement!"

After a sigh, you gently close the door and return to the lounge. One of your children asks "Who was that?" "Just someone who was confused" you reply, and get back to the love of your family.

I don't imagine anyone, on their death-bed, would wish they'd hired that coach who pumped them up more and helped them achieve more extraordinary results...

I personally think people are much more grateful for discovering how they really experience life and developing a deeper understanding of the nature of being human. From that they often experience more love, peace and understanding of others, deeper connections and a deeper happiness beyond any circumstances. Counter-intuitively, perhaps, it is from this place people seem to experience success that they often describe as effortless, simply because they no longer holding on to ideas of who or what they are, and are then free to be in the flow of life.

A client summed up our work together beautifully:

"Phil showed me how to recognise the deeper aspects of myself, to be more authentic, to see past my excuses, to be in joy, to be love and in love with all things."

Whilst I have helped many people grow their businesses, these have been by-products of becoming deeply connected to themselves beyond any ideas, concepts or conditioning. Loosening their grip on their ideas and beliefs and subsequently becoming deeply connected to and understanding love.

My favourite client stories remain those where broken family relationships and friendships have been restored to joyful loving ones, where my clients feel in love with life.

Feedback such as 'I find myself loving my family more' and 'I feel like I'm doing less work yet my business is thriving, AND I get to spend more time with my wife' inspires me more than any dollars.

Ultimately, it seems, success always comes down to how much we loved.

# How the Goddess of Ego Hides You from You

One thing I have seen more and more over the last few years that is truly helpful for people, is to help them see the role that ideas, concepts and beliefs play in their experience of life. Some suggest helping people understand their 'true essence', a term I have used, yet there is danger in even that becoming unhelpful since it can encourage people to look for just another belief or concept, and in many cases proliferate further suffering.

To have people search inside themselves for concepts such as goddesses of compassion or abundance, or examine their levels of masculinity and femininity with a view to change, however well intended, is like holding up a mirror to someone that has a picture already drawn on it. Whilst it is suggested that the attributes of these ideals are within us all, what they have people do is look for aspects of themselves in a form that may not be true for them, thereby inspiring a feeling of lacking.

So many times I've seen and heard comments such as "I struggle so much with this" or "I've lived all my life in this unhealthy way." Yet, who's to say it is something for you to struggle with or that it is unhealthy? Coach's unconscious mission accompli - you feel there is something you need to work on to be healthy, you enlist the help of the coach... It all makes for a great marketing strategy, particularly in a culture of fear and self-rejection.

Concepts are held up to us like the proliferation of a disease, subliminally suggesting there is something wrong with us, despite assuring us there is nothing wrong with us, all we need do is find our inner goddess of moon and nature whilst excreting unicorn honeyed-milk in a perfectly balanced masculine and feminine expression of a mission greater than world peace to be worthy of God...

Enough! Please, enough!

These will NEVER help you see you.

Here's the rub: All the time I am searching in myself for some conceptual ideas of who I think I am or need to be, I am looking for a part of me that only exists in thought. I am actually only ever looking for another part of my ego.

Holding up some conceptual idea of who you are, however well intended, points us away from the freedom that is available to us all, and invariably has us feel that we're either not enough or not being ourselves, until we find that concept that we seek. Of course, we can never truly find it, it's like looking for the ocean in a picture of the ocean.

As long as you search for something that does not exist I guarantee you will never find it. All we end up doing is creating a more complex conceptual version of ourselves, creating another set of beliefs about ourselves that limit us in the same way as all formed beliefs do.

And it's exhausting!!

Oh, to relinquish all that work... to give up all that relates to blame, shame and guilt... to give in to allow the peace of all that we already are without mirrors, drawings, concepts and the craziness of head-full searches within for a self that doesn't even exist.

What's it like to be you when you're not trying to be somebody, even yourself?

You are not a goddess, mermaid, unicorn, alpha-metrosexual-perfect-equilibrium of masculine and feminine.

You are beyond all these ideas, before all these concepts are formed. It is in this direction and this direction only, before form, that you need consider to discover the love that is freely available to you when you allow the full natural expression of yourself.

It is only ever thinking we need to be different that keeps us away from the beauty that we already are. This thinking and exploration ignores the undefinable essence of us that awaits us beyond these ideas, and is the source of all suffering. If you are being encouraged to look in the direction of these concepts you are being directed to suffering.

I invite you to relinquish the exploration of such concepts, they are only ever outside of you and keep you from you, even if you feel you recognise aspects of these concepts within you. The ego so often recognises itself, especially when listed on a menu of fear.

At most, hold these concepts loosely, as observations, in the same way you may observe a bird sweeping across the sky, or the petals of a rose blowing in the wind. And know that the place from which the bird and the rose emerge is the same place within you from which all emerges. No comparison, no analysis, no mermaid cloak or other thinking required.

You are not a concept. You are the energy of pure infinite potentiality, expressing perfectly in any moment. There is no work for you to do to be you. You don't need to find you or even your true essence to be more you.

There really is nothing for you to do.

Or as one of my friends put it - just live ya life!

# Connected

I'm always surprised, and at the same time reassured, how connected and in alignment we can be with some people, even though, physically, we may be separated by many miles, ideas opinions and outlook. Some connections are beyond this physical realm, for sure, yet leak into it, in ways demonstrating and leaving clues to that connection that can be disputed, yet, once we see, are irrefutable.

I wonder what might be available to us if we truly embraced these connections, even if they go against many ideas, ideals and intellectual understandings we have of this worldly realm?...

We can call such evidence of connections coincidence, or 'accidents' but, of course, it's often suggested 'there are no accidents,' as I was reminded by a dear friend recently. What if this all is set up for us?...

When I was younger I'd describe much of my thinking and outlook on life as scientific. Yet, as I've explored human behaviour over the last 20 years or so, and particularly our spiritual nature over the last 12 years, it's increasingly obvious to me there is more to this condition of being human than our little minds can muster. We are connected in ways beyond our comprehension.

We are all dancing in the energy of life and love. There is a mystery to this that we might ignore. Yet, it seems to me, embracing it invites us into possibilities of beautiful unions across our interpretation of physical and spiritual realms. Perhaps the ultimate union back to oneself. I like that idea.

Sometimes I think maybe I am just dreaming... and maybe being able to send dreams, thinking of and sharing exactly the same things at the same times, are just part of a coincidental dream... Maybe this is all one big dream.

Yet some things we see cannot be unseen. And sometimes seeing only takes a glimpse.

As Dr Wayne Dyer often said, we are Spiritual Beings having a human experience. And it's very clear to me that, underneath this human experience, we are connected in ways that may look mysterious to the human mind, yet make complete sense beyond our physical realm.

Once we're open to really seeing this, we get to see more of the everyday miracles that become kind of matter-of-fact. 'Of course!' I find myself exclaiming, when I see evidence of such connections. Of course! How could I ever doubt it?

Ah yes... doubt... my little indicator I am attempting to separate myself from love.

To all of you reading this, I love you, I hope you feel that. And to those that don't, won't read this, I also know you can feel my love. In the quiet moments you let it in.

The denial of truth doesn't make it untrue. My truth is I feel you. There is no separation. And I love you. Mind, body & spirit.

# Resentment

You cannot harbour resentment in one part of your life and be truly, deeply happy in another. True happiness is the heart that holds no resentment, the crystal clear untainted by drops of red. At least, this is how it has appeared to me and many of my clients.

I've coached numerous people who have harboured some form of resentment in one area of their life, and it leaks into all others, like a toxic chemical. The company director struggling to connect with his team until he released resentment around a broken down friendship, the manager unable to get a promotion until she released resentment around a family situation...

Happiness is the greatest lubricant in life, yet it is not fully available to us whilst we obstruct its natural flow and energy by holding grievances and resentment. Those little drops of red ink cloud the whole glass of water.

There is a path, an understanding available to all of us that can help us let go of our resentments and grievances. It's something I've explored for many years, and has played a big part in being open to being able to reconnect with my Dad. And I see the benefits in all areas of my life, including my business and flow of money. In some respects that looks like a miracle, and also makes complete sense.

Once I am open to one miracle, I am open to all miracles. Once I am open to love in one aspect of my life I can be open to love in all aspects of my life.

Once my glass of water is clear, it is reflected in all aspects of my life...

# Parenting Friendship

"I wish I had a relationship with my son like you have with yours."

I've heard this quite a few times during the last twenty years. Naturally I feel some pride, but I also always feel a tinge of sadness too.

Simply because to have the kind of relationship which we both describe as 'best friends' is generally much easier than the people who state this desire seem to believe.

For me it was a very simple shift. I remember the exact moment I chose to no longer be the policing, authoritarian parent and instead chose to BE my son's best friend. There is nothing complicated about that, if you want someone's friendship, be their friend.

Sadly, we've all seen it; parents berating their children, issuing demanding instructions, dictating what they should or shouldn't do next, and speaking to them in ways that they would never dream of talking to their best friends.

If you talk to your child aggressively, put very simply, they will develop an aggressive relationship with you. If you speak to your child lovingly, with understanding, they will develop a loving and understanding relationship with you.

If you are constantly at war with your child, particularly with a young child who has very little other experience of the world, they will see the world as a war zone.

In reality, once I had made the choice to be my son's friend, life became much more pleasant and easier. Seeing other parents be at war with their children and struggle through their idea of their version of parenthood saddens me because living that way is both unnecessary and the most difficult path to take. Once I had chosen friendship over what might be described as 'traditional parenthood' (in my opinion archaic and draconian parenthood), being with my son was effortless.

Have you ever considered which is more enjoyable, being with your loving and understanding friends, or having an argument with someone who rarely agrees with you?

The most natural thing for any of us to do when we feel either threatened or attacked is to either get defensive or attack back, especially when we are children and are still developing the social skills of survival.

If someone spoke to you, yes you the parent, saying things like "what are you doing now?" or "stop that! come here now!" in a very demanding voice, would you feel compelled to comply, and endeared to be helpful to that person? Yet, time and time again, this is the kind of language I hear some parents using with their children. A barrage of constant instructions, interrogation, exclamations, as if everything the child is doing is vindictive and wrong. No attempt is ever made to understand the child's thinking, to deeply connect and understand them so that they can be pointed towards love.

All children's behaviour is innocent and is only ever a reflection of how they see the world. They learn how to see that world mostly from their parents. If they see the world as antagonistic that is indeed how they will behave.

Children learn to think the whole world is against them if the majority of the communication they have with their parents is aggressive, authoritarian, and instructive. When our children are allowed to freely express themselves, to explore, are appreciated and encouraged and understood, they learn to see the world as cooperative and supportive and understanding, and in turn mirror back cooperative and supportive behaviour.

Gandhi really did teach us so much from what is my most favourite quote:

'Be the change you wish to see in the world.'

If you want to have the kind of relationship with your child that is predominantly one of friendship there is only one very simple way of creating that:

Be that child's best friend. Be that child's most supportive, most encouraging, most understanding, most patient, most accepting, most fun, most approachable, most trustworthy, most trusting, most connected, most affectionate and most loving best friend.

*In every moment you are an expression of your 'true essence', including your compelling yet ultimately unnecessary quest for it.*

# The Happy Tool of Money

'Dear God, I hear that fame and fortune won't bring me happiness, but please let me find out for myself.'

We see it all around us - the belief proliferated that more of something, often money, will bring a particular feeling, often happiness.

But that's not how life really works.

Money in particular is the subject of much theory and deliberation regarding happiness. Yet we only have to pick up a celebrity magazine or read about financially wealthy people to see they are no more happy than most of us. Having coached both millionaires and people in financial poverty, it's plainly obvious to me that there is no correlation between money and happiness.

Money in and of itself cannot bring any feeling, just like anything outside of us cannot help us feel anything. But it is a great tool for exchanging value of service and therefore opening up avenues of more options.

So if you are predominantly unhappy, money will help you explore more ways to discover and show you that. And yes, it can help you invest in exploring ways to discover how to reconnect with your innate happiness. Perhaps its most worthwhile use.

But it's never the money that brings happiness, it only enables you to explore more options to discover the truth about happiness.

Money is a great tool. That's all.

A very useful one, and one I LOVE to use abundantly and often. But just a tool, all the same.

# Do I Believe My Beliefs?

*Whatever you believe to be true you will experience as true.*

Do I believe the world to be kind or unkind?

Do I believe people to be good or bad?

Do I believe people are liars or honest?

Do I believe there is no purpose to life, or that there is something deeper?

Do I believe whatever I'm doing is fun or boring?

Do I believe someone loves me, or that they don't?

Do I believe life/the universe/God/a greater intelligence supports me, or it's all baloney?

Do I believe in soulmates or twin-flames?

Do I believe in love at first sight?

Do I believe in love?

Do I believe my beliefs?

This final question can open us up to our true liberation. Once we see that our experience of life depends, not so much on what we think and believe, but our relationship to what we think and believe, we can become free from our beliefs.

Free from, rather than free of our beliefs. As far as I can tell, humans entertain beliefs, they are a natural part of how we interpret and look to navigate and understand the world. Yet, when we see that all our beliefs are imagined, exist only in thought, our relationship to any of our beliefs can change, our hold onto our beliefs often softens as we see their made-up nature and that they only exist as thought.

And in that softening, our deeper experience of life seems to depend less on what we think we know, but what we simply see as thinking that we know.

At least, that's how it looks to me...

# Transformed Relationships.
# Transformed Lives.

"My sister called me just to see how I am. She hasn't done that in years!"

"On a call today, my Mum used a term of endearment with me she hasn't used since I was a kid. We're definitely closer now."

"(After falling out a few years ago and not returning any calls or texts since), my friend just contacted me out of the blue. It is a miracle."

"My parents have gone from avoiding visiting me completely to popping round all the time."

"We've explored some new things in bed for the first time, definitely because of our increased trust and intimacy."

"We simply don't argue anymore. Sure, we disagree, but there are no longer arguments about our differences, if anything, we see the humour in them."

"This working relationship is now exactly that - a working relationship!"

I've heard a version of all of these a number of times over the last couple of years. They are all examples of the type of feedback I've been getting from clients about their relationships and how their lives have changed during and after our time together.

Whilst there is often a focus on relationships in our conversations, it is certainly not always the case. We explore all things in life and business, and of course as part of any exploration the role of relationships is unavoidable.

It's not just relationships that change; clients get promotions, bonuses and raises, unexpected job offers, experience business growth and opportunities, and a whole bunch of other miracles. Yet, perhaps all these things come about because of how their relationships change. So much suddenly seems to become possible, particularly when our relationship with our own beliefs and our own thinking changes.

*When our relationship with our thinking is transformed, our relationship with life and everything and everyone in it, is also transformed.*

As I reflect on the experiences of my clients over the last few years, it is the impact on their personal and business relationships that touch me the most. Sure, big bonuses, promotions and business growth are great, we celebrate those and it is those that often help us to continue to work together. But it is the often-smaller changes that all add up to transforming their experiences of the people around them, and hence their experience of life, that truly make our time together beautiful, miraculous, amazing. Priceless.

This weekend, when visiting my Dad, he once again sat on the same sofa as me, something he never used to do. I'm sure he doesn't even notice, yet I feel it, his manifestation of feeling closer to me as a result of our understanding each other and deeper connection.

If my relationship with my Dad can be transformed in this way, if the seemingly broken relationships some of my clients have had can be transformed, I have no doubts at all that the same is possible for anyone. For anyone willing to explore past their current way of seeing, for anyone open to new understanding. For anyone willing to love.

# Travelling to Me

For as long as I can remember, I've always wanted to travel the world. That desire has often taken a back-seat, hidden beneath commitments of bringing up a family and illusionary edges to what I've believed is possible. But the mystery and adventure of it remains compelling, drawing me into lands and experiences not yet even dreamed.

At the same time I've always felt I'm searching for something in life. Searching and waiting. Often I've been clear what that is, other times I've just lived with the emptiness of its absence.

In recent years I've seen how these two things were previously linked in some way. Part of the reason I've wanted to travel had been a faint hope of finding what I've been looking for 'out there.' A never-ending quest, fuelled by the emptiness and blindness to what has always been within me. Always somehow waiting for it to find me.

I'd dreamt of meeting and finding that thing out on the road, perhaps in foreign lands and beaches. A chance meeting in a roadside cafe.

What is it I'd been looking for? Hoping for? Waiting for?

Connection. A deep feeling of loving, belonging, acceptance and connection.

And fun too!

Until recently, that feeling also remained a dream. But like a forbidden fruit, I have tasted beautiful moments of that life-long-craved connection, when everything around us stops and nothing else exists outside of the experience of us. A spiritual communion played in a physical realm of unity.

Or more simply, moments when nothing else at all mattered. Time, space, location, vocation, bank balances, temperatures, weather and tides, all an irrelevance outside of our beautiful meeting of souls.

And the times it showed up, it did so unexpectedly, when I wasn't waiting and right where I always was. I didn't have to go anywhere, do anything, or try and be anyone. In fact, it showed up whilst I was simply living being who I already am. In some ways it looks like it showed up when I had released any attachment I ever had to finding it. Not a giving up hope, but a surrendering to what is here now and allowing myself to be present to now.

Whilst those moments may have been brief, often short lived under circumstances I would prefer to be different, they have reminded me that what I have always desired in life is possible, and whilst I do still want to travel and see as much of the world as my time here will allow, I no longer feel the need to do that as part of a deeper search for something that had often felt both improbable and impossible.

And even more recently, in even more briefer moments, I have seen the source of that beautiful feeling of connection. Oh, how the gloriously romantic in me wants to believe it can only come from 'the one.' Yet, there's been a deeper revealing of what it means to feel connected.

One of my mentors suggests that all each of us ever wants is an experience of our own heart, and in those moments of connection it feels like the image I often hold of myself disappears into the love of my heart. Of course, as a regular human being, I want to share such beautiful experiences, especially with someone with whom I'm intimate and love. But the source of those experiences is not from another, it is in the recognition of who I am and my own heart.

When I've thought that I needed someone I have suffered, simply because that someone cannot fulfil that which is within me.

When I truly see me and all that I am, I am fulfilled. Only I can love me the way I want to be loved, because I am the love that I think I want.

In the times of deeper connection all travel and going someplace else takes on a different meaning. It's not the desperate longing it once was, but a sense of adventure to be shared. And its importance to me lessens as I hold dear the connection that I was searching for within that longing to travel.

So, to you, my dear 'soulmate', my dearest friend, partner, lover, accomplice in all adventures, yes I want you with me, I want to take the rest of this journey with you, to travel not only around the world but through this beautifully rich experience of life. Yes, come with me.

Come and join me, give life and love with me. It is this giving that is the sweetest joy of life.

My relationship with you will be one of giving and receiving, a dance of trust and knowing ourselves and each other.

I have seen me and know who I am and know what I have to give, with a clarity I've not felt before, whether you choose to see me or not. Who I am is not dependent on you and I don't need you. But I do want you and want to give us to us.

In essence the search and the wait is over.

Seeing myself came in a single moment of realisation, and in that moment I realised, I wasn't waiting for you, I was waiting for me.

*What might you do differently today if you just let in a little more love?*

# Reflecting on Denying Me

At the weekend, whilst sitting outside the house where my grandparents spent their entire marriage of over seventy years together, I spent a few minutes reflecting on my life. As I sat there quietly, paused, remembering so many good times, a lump came to my throat. But not for the loss of, or indeed gratitude for my grandparents, but the loss of something much deeper within me.

Looking at that house and recalling so many wonderful times there as a child, I remembered the innocence of a childhood uninhibited and uncontaminated by broken marriages, broken relationships, broken or failed businesses, uncontaminated by broken dreams. The innocence of a dreamy childhood uncontaminated by so many experiences of life as an adult.

That lump in my throat was for all those years I was lost, spent in relationships I didn't want to be in, that were not good for me, that had me be the subject of abuse, where there was a lack of self-love, kindness and connection. A lump in my throat for so many adult years doing work I didn't want to do, just to survive, just to get through each day and each week, through to each months pay check and all the pay checks between each Christmas, each year.

I felt a mixture of appreciation and sadness at so many years of this life already lived. Like many of us, so many of those years I would, of course, have lived differently with the wisdom those experiences brought, such is the paradox of life, and of course, life simply doesn't work that way.

I rarely feel regret, I have already lived a very full life, one for which I'm enormously grateful, and have been privileged to have participated in bringing up a family, and travelled to many beautiful parts of this world.

But the lump in my throat, reflecting outside that house at the weekend, brought a message that choked me inside.

'Don't settle!'

Don't settle for less than what you want, irrespective of whether you believe you can have it. So many times in my life I thought 'well this is as good as it gets.' And it never was. In fact, mostly it was never even as good as I was trying to tell myself it was.

'Don't settle!' - Such a clear message from the last thirty years of my life.

My experiences of marriage relationships that didn't 'work out' has helped me see very clearly what kind of relationship I want and all that I bring. Similarly, whilst I was very successful in my twenty-six year corporate career, it's only in the last seven years or so that I have felt I am very much in my zone of genius and living into the purpose of my life.

It's taken me this long to get real honest about what I want, and this long to say 'fuck it!' to any thoughts around it not being possible. In any case, how could I know?

For many years I dared not even look deeply into what I wanted, in my relationships or my vocation. I settled for what I thought was possible and allowed my inner desires for freedom, love, exploration, creation, affection and kindness, to be quelled by those illusionary edges of 'this is as good as it gets.'

Fuck that!

I have clarity about what I want in life and how I want my life to be like never before. Many things have become crystal clear to me over the past few years, and I see that what I want IS possible because of who I am!

I am part of the infinite creative potential of the universe.

So instead of settling, what if we opened our hearts to what we really want and allowed those desires out into the world, without the illusionary limits of what we believe is possible?

My grandparents lived an incredibly simple life, loved each other and cared about each other dearly, and were so devoted to each other. It's a very different world now to what it was for them seventy, fifty, even twenty years ago.

Yet it's not that less is possible now; more is possible. We live in a world where travel is easier than it's ever been, where it's easier to connect with people than it's ever been, it's easier to meet people all over the world than it's ever been. Maybe there is a downside in that it does, at times to me at least, seem it is more difficult to connect with people local to us, in our own towns and cities, without resorting to virtual connections in the online world. People seem to be at home on their computers or, when out and about, on their smartphones.

But overall I believe the world today brings potential to our fingertips in ways that my Grandparents couldn't even conceive. So much is possible now, more than we can ever know. So much help and support is also available to us now. We have a coaching profession, truly one of the most beautiful professions in the world.

I have a renewed determination to make this next phase of my life the best it's ever been. For the first time in my life I am feeling, with depth, that I am deserving of the love I want, and know it is me that has to give that to me. And it is me that can bring love into everything I do, my relationships and my work. I see time and time again, with my clients and in my own life, that anything really is possible. I'm done with settling for less.

All of us use our fears to keep us safe, yet for many of us that also means keeping ourselves from what we really want and what is here for us. None of us has to settle for a dead relationship or dead-end job. We have the creative potential of the universe flowing through us. We have the creative power and wisdom of love available to us, always.

We must listen to love, and start by listening to what it is we would love to do, and how we would truly love our life to be. Just as my Grandparents did.

Not to listen to fears and false beliefs of limitation, but to get real honest about our desires and to listen to love. This is what I am here to help people see and do. This is what it is to truly love ourselves.

Thank you, dear Grandma & Pop.

# My Selfish Nobility

A few years ago, whilst in Las Vegas, I went with a friend to a local church and was very amused by the words to one of the songs the congregation sang. It was very jovial and upbeat, and the words were along the lines of 'Our God is greater, our God is bigger.' Those words of separation and division struck me as being totally misaligned with everything that church stood for.

Ideas of division are often used as an attention grabber on social media. 'Great coaches do this' or 'not so great coaches do this instead. 'Great leaders do this' and 'not so great leaders do this instead.'

By the same token, we also see people sharing their vision of God as a truth. Now of course, we don't say at the start of every post or article 'this is my opinion,' it goes unsaid. And whilst that is all anything that we write or share can be, it is also often forgotten. This chapter is another of those "This is how I perceive it' or 'This is how I see it.' It can be helpful to keep this in mind. 'This is how I see the world.' That's all I've got.

Some of the things people write look like absolute baloney to me, probably at times to you too. Yet I recognise they are sharing an opinion that is no less or indeed no more valid than mine. Other times I think something is genius, 'Yes! That's how it is! Truth at last!' What's actually happening is I am noticing their thinking and beliefs are similar to mine. That's all it ever is. Personal thinking, personal perception, personal understanding.

I was recently discussing a social media post with someone, a post that ignited much debate. Yet if I read these things and keep in mind that much of what is said really comes down to a person's beliefs of what and who God is and the role that God plays in the universe, it becomes easier for me to look at such posts subjectively, as all these things are.

In a similar vein, this morning I see an idea that if you ask God, or the universe, or spirit, for something that is personal, for your own benefit, it is much less likely to be fulfilled than any impersonal request that is for a greater good, or for some benefit other than my own. Our requests and prayers, apparently, are more likely to be met and fulfilled if they are for an impersonal good. Again, the premise here is a belief in who or what God is and the role that God plays, and whilst to some it may seem so true it is worthy of a fist-bump or high-five, they are only ever an opinion based on that person's thinking and beliefs, in turn perhaps based on their own observations. 'Here's how it looks to me.'

I ask most of my guests on my podcast, The Coaching Life, 'for you what is the purpose of your coaching?' I asked this to my dear friend Mark Silverman recently, and he gave the most beautiful answer.

He said 'My job is to introduce people to God, whoever that is for them.'

Those last five words are absolutely crucial as a coach. Those five words are what differentiate me as a coach, facilitator and explorer from a preacher and teacher. I have nothing to teach you, only to offer myself as a tour guide on an exploration and journey of discovering of what is true for you. Sure, there are things I have 'seen' that you may also like to see, but whatever that is, whatever you see will be very personal to you. It may look the same for me, sometimes, but it will always be personal to you.

It may look like a universal truth, but your experience of that truth will always be personal to you.

My opinion will be irrelevant. And I notice my own opinion around this idea that personal requests are less likely to be fulfilled than impersonal requests is also heavily laced with my own experience and beliefs.

As far as I can tell there is no such thing as an impersonal request. Despite the extent of people's understanding of the inside nature of life, in my twenty one years of studying human behaviour and fifteen years coaching, I've yet to meet anyone who ever does anything for a reason other than to feel better. Often very noble reasons are given, 'I want to coach because I want to change the world and make it a better, safer, more loving place.' Yet the only reason, underneath all those noble ones, is always a desire to feel better, most often to feel better about ourselves.

Underneath all the nobility, we do stuff because it feels good to do it. Therefore, all impersonal requests are personal.

But then, my feeling better, happier, more in touch with love, vibrating at a higher frequency, however we want to describe it, makes the world a better place. Howard Thurman said "Don't ask yourself what the world needs. Ask yourself what makes you come alive, and go do that, because what the world needs is people who have come alive." In that respect, there is no such thing as a personal request. All requests and prayers are for a greater good.

To suggest there is a difference between personal and impersonal requests implies there is a judgment made by God, Spirit, the Universe. The idea of a God passing judgment on prayers and requests to ascertain if they are worthy seems like an archaic idea to me, and is not one to which I subscribe. It in no way aligns with my own belief of what many call God - Love. Love is the absence of judgment.

There is no need to preach separation and division in this respect. This is my opinion. Through my own exploration I have got more in touch with what God, Spirit, Love is to me. I'll not preach that to you, only share how I see it. That is all any of us can ever do. Hence I could never suggest that if you don't see things the same way as me, you are not a great coach, or a great leader, or a great teacher, or indeed a great anything. You too are an expression of Love. Some would say an expression of God.

As a coach I ask many 'What if?' questions. 'What if that were not true?' 'What if that were true?' What if greatness is not something you are but something that channels through you? What if there is no difference between personal and impersonal? What if you are always an expression of God? What if you asking is indeed God asking of herself? What if? What feels true for you?

Coaching, for me, the way I see it, is to help you explore and discover, not what is true for me or indeed my version of God, but what is true for you, and who God is for you. As a coach I'll help you create whatever you want to create in the world.

And I'll do that with love, as an expression of Love, because doing so feels good, really really good, however great, personal or impersonal that is.

# The Dance of Thoughts.

Some mornings I wake up almost in tears because of how beautiful my life seems.

Some mornings I wake up almost in tears because of how much of a mess my life seems.

Not much changes between these mornings.

\* \* \* \* \* \*

"May I please just have permission to leave?

I mean... this mostly sucks and the only reason I seem to stay is to prevent loved ones from suffering loss. That's one hell of a sacrifice. I could be home by now, in infinite peace. Yet, I'm supposed to stay because my going would hurt others? Ironic, in a way, since one thing I've learnt is that any sacrifice is an attempt to separate ourselves from love. Well, listen... I want to return to love, from whence we came, sooner rather than later, instead of enduring this daily grind of supposed illusionary individuality.

This life is just too painful, meaningless, alone. May I leave now? Just go home. Return to source by my own choosing.

Really, the only thing keeping me here seems to be to prevent others from suffering. I'm not afraid to go. The more I understand it, it's where we're meant to be, where we'll all end up anyways, and what does it matter if infinity starts a few years early for me?"

\* \* \* \* \* \*

"That ant is amazing. Grappling with that crumb. See how it's actually bigger than him. Is he actually going to be able to carry it? What a miracle he is. And that glint of sun that splits into rainbow colours through the edge of that glass. Isn't sunshine on raindrops beautiful?

Looking at the globe in the corner of the room, there's so many countries I want to explore. I have so many lovely friends in the U.S. Aren't airplanes amazing? I've flown over two hundred times, but it feels like I'm overdue a flight somewhere. Maybe get that Zakynthos flight booked sooner rather than later...

Remembering her smile. So slight, a smile with knowing. I hope this memory lasts forever, and is joined by many more.

I'd happily watch and listen all day...

Sitting here, just observing life, there is so much in it. So much to explore. So much going on we never seem to even notice.

Do you have any idea how many unread books are on my kindle?

Oh, the ant has left the crumb.

So much here I want to see, touch, feel. So much life still to live.

What a beautiful life."

* * * * * *

The dance of random, neutral thoughts passing through the mind of a human being. Sometimes feeling consumed by the dance, other times just watching it. Sometimes swimming in the river, other times watching the stream. Noticing the constant flow and changes as thoughts pass freely. Occasionally one shows up that seems to have some significance. Other times the idea of significance reveals itself as a thought too.

Neither of these trains of thoughts have any inherent meaning. Sometimes it feels like they do, as another layer of thinking about them arrives. And as meaning is also seen as being made of the same stuff, being made of thought, it too seems to dissolve and pass.

Horror movies, then gentle meadows of bouncy rabbits and rainbows, and everything else imagined in between. Meaningless, even with perceived meaning.

Seeing this, knowing all these thoughts pass through, uninhibited if we let them, noticing them rather than giving credence to them, simply noticing them, we are free.

# Slowing Down to Peace and Love

On my way home from St. Patrick Day celebrations on Saturday evening, walking down a small alleyway, I came across a man shouting and finger pointing very aggressively at a woman, almost pinning her against the wall.

I immediately called out to him 'whoa, whoa, let's slow down here.' Predictably, he turned very angrily towards me, telling me to mind my own business, laced with a few other choice words. I repeated to him 'I'm just suggesting that we all just slow down a little and take a few breathes.'

He then walked off, throwing a few other insults, and the woman thanked me. I asked if she wanted to call anyone, or get a cup of tea at the bar next door, and she said she had to go, she was staying in a room with the guy just nearby. Asking once again if she was okay, and her insisting she was, we parted. When I got to the front of the building I explained what had happened to the security team and asked that they go check on her.

Reflecting on this I notice I felt no fear at all, only compassion for both of them. I, too, have felt that anger, and I, too, have been the subject of physical abuse. I also notice that what occurred to me in that moment, was not to suggest he calmed down, (I'm not sure that, in the entire history of people being told to calm down anyone has ever calmed down by being told to calm down...) but to suggest he SLOWED down. Maybe there is no difference, maybe simply my presence helped and nothing more, or maybe it was a difference subtle enough, I'll never know.

But it reminded me of the simplicity of seeing any uncomfortable emotion as an invitation to slow down. Not necessarily to physically slow down, but to allow our thinking to slow down, to allow some space for a little more sense to appear out of the confusion of muddy thinking.

In those moments, that guy was completely indulged in his thinking, drowning in it, allowing his rage inside to manifest in actions outside, there being zero space between his thinking and his actions.

It is in slowing down that we allow the space to see our thinking for what it is. "It seemed like a good idea at the time" often dissolving into an alternative, more peaceful and loving version.

I'm grateful I showed up when I did, although it can never be known what might have happened otherwise, and I am even more grateful for the times I get to see the illusionary and transient nature of our thinking, and get to remember what reveals itself when we allow our thinking to slow and fall away.

Remembering love is always there, whatever we're believing, in any moment, helps us to allow other options to appear, even when the waters are muddy. As Byron Katie says, if we're not feeling love, we're confused.

I am filled with compassion for anyone feeling so confused as to be consumed by their feelings of anger, and for anyone subjected to behaviours born out of that confusion and distraction from love.

And I'm super grateful for all my teachers and mentors over the last twenty years that have helped me see and understand a little more about the nature of the human experience, and the nature of love.

# Preparing to be Unprepared

"How much preparation do you do before coaching calls?"

I was asked a version of this question by a client this morning, and have seen it asked and debated on social media.

When I started coaching professionally in 2005, I did no preparation at all. The conversations were few and far between, and mostly with family, friends, friends of family, friends of friends, very small fees, and I mostly knew a little about the person I was talking with. Looking back, I had no idea what I was doing, just curiosity and a sense of a direction I wanted to encourage my clients to look. This might seem like unconscious incompetence, yet on reflection there was greater competence there than first appears.

Through some of my training and mentoring I'd been inspired to research everything there is to know about my clients, not just to understand what they are capable of, but, as was taught unashamedly, to impress them. "Didn't you win the young entrepreneur of the year award three times in high-school for your tuck shop business that was actually an undercover illicit tobacco importing operation?"

"Wow, you've certainly done your homework, dear Mr Coach, here's two hundred grand!"

I was never comfortable with this. I always know my clients are capable of almost anything, and there was an aspect to this research that always felt distasteful, irrelevant, and creepy.

In any case, why do I need to know so much about my clients and all the stories they have enacted in their life if my role as a coach is to help them see what is possible beyond all their stories?

This came up in one of the last such training events I attended in LA late 2014, where someone in the team I was leading suggested she wanted to find a coach who was also a single Mom, 'so that she will understand all the challenges that entails.' I suggested that, whilst that may be true, she might be better served by someone who had absolutely no idea what it was like to be such a Mom, since they would be far less likely to buy into any bullshit stories around it.

The more I understand about what it is to be human and the infinite potential of which we are all part, the less I need to know about my clients. In understanding we all see life through stories I can remain ignorant of the content of them. And nowadays, often beyond an initial level of amusement and fascination, I'm generally not so interested.

As far as preparation goes, I need to know nothing about my client over and above what I already know of what it means to be human, plus maybe some points we may have discussed on a previous call, such as committed actions. (I'm not in any way an accountability coach, but I am always fascinated and curious when a client commits to something which they then do not do.)

It seems the best preparation I can undertake prior to any session is to allow myself to be present and drop any notion of 'me,' including any stories 'I' may have entertained about my client. That used to be a 5 or 10 minute meditation, but more recently is simply a bathroom visit and a glass of water so as not to get distracted by my body.

Then instead of unconscious incompetence, or indeed any level of personal competence, I get to show up, present, conscious, without any preconceived notions of knowing, and allow loving curiosity to guide us to wherever we're to go.

*Live like you're gorgeous.*
*Because you are.*

# Who Why Bananas

'Instead of asking why, find your who.'

'Instead of asking who am I, find your why.'

Both of these statements are seen around coaching circles, and both simply suggest you shift focus from one concept to another

I can discover (fabricate) a 'who' that feels good and therefore I create some feeling of freedom

I can discover (fabricate) a 'why' that feels good and therefore I create some feeling of freedom.

An outside-in presentation of inside-out.

The energy that creates the feeling of freedom for each statement is made of the same stuff.

I invite you to consider another approach, (yes, in itself a concept, but that's all we've got) - that of seeing all concepts and ideas as made up. No more work to discover your why, no more work to discover your who, no more work about yourself, the universe, oneness, purpose, true self, bananas, or God.

No need to do any of it... and then the search simply becomes a game you either choose to participate in for fun and enjoyment, or not.

Imagine just doing stuff for fun and enjoyment!

Ah, the freedom in that...

# Things Work Out

Whatever you have going on in your life right now, if you are suffering or feeling heartbroken, I send you love.

My own experiences have taught me so much that my heart bursts open with compassion at the thought of your pain.

I attempted suicide and took an overdose in my twenties, early in my thirties found myself completely disorientated upon the discovery of unfaithfulness in my marriage and then the break up of the family to which I had given my all for more than ten years. In my forties, relationship heartbreak, and even very recently, in the last few days, an event that some might describe as traumatising.

I understand what it's like to feel depressed, broken and lost, suicidal. At least, I understand my version of them...

Yet I have a deeper sense of love and peace than I've ever felt. A lightness and flow in life that, when I remember, (which is certainly not all the time!) reminds me of these three words:

***Things work out.***

That doesn't mean I don't get upset, angry, or feel emotional pain. It doesn't mean I don't feel fear, occasionally a sense of apprehension, or even momentary bat-shit scared, even traumatised.

What it means is that I'm no longer attempting to avoid these experiences, at least not to the extent I may have done in my twenties.

You've probably seen it written a thousand times, it is our resisting the flow of life that prolongs our suffering. It looks to me that my attempts to avoid 'bad' experiences has me avoid 'good' ones too. We can't numb ourselves to fear and sadness without numbing ourselves to all life has to offer, including love and happiness.

What I see, time and time again, in myself and in many others, is an incredible resilience. However broken our dreams, however broken we feel, we have an incredible capacity to carry on and recover.

Surely recovering is the most badass thing that humans do!

Not much looks real to me nowadays, I'm increasingly seeing the made-up nature of everything in life. But this one thing, our resilience, looks very real to me, certainly more real than any suffering I have experienced, since, for the most part, I am still here and my suffering is not.

In the absence of our resistance to experiences, our innate ability to recover does its thing, whatever that is, and we get through, things work out, and very often we grow in ways we may not have without these experiences.

During a particularly tough time a couple of years ago I was fortunate to have friends who were simply with me, loving me, without trying to change my experience, knowing that within me was the capacity to recover, naturally.

'I know' they told me, as I shared my pain.

And I could sense they did know, that they knew something I was simply not seeing at the time - things would change, how I felt would change, how I was seeing life would change, and there really was nothing I needed to do for that to happen.

Recovery was inevitable.

And one day I woke up and simply noticed, 'Aha yes, I do feel different.' I can't tell you what I did because whatever it was, things changed, I recovered. Despite whatever I did.

Life itself seemed to take care of the 'how.'

If we're suffering all we need know is that however we feel and however things look right now, that can and invariably will change. How that change might look and feel, I can't tell you, I just know it will.

Actually, we don't even need to know this. It just happens.

Reflecting on the impermanence of absolutely everything, seeing the transient nature of even the most painful of questions such as 'How on earth am I ever going to get through this?' - all I know is that we can. Peace and love seems to be relentless in finding a way to come back through us even after the most harrowing and painful experiences.

And of course, such is our experience of life that when we are in the mire of it all, this can look like absolute bullshit. I get it.

So, whatever is going on in your life right now, particularly if it sucks, it's painful, you wish with all your might it were different, I know. I know.

I love you.

And irrespective of whether you believe it, things will work out.

# A Spiritual Hoodwink

'Once you discover who you are, you're home.'

'Just keeping looking in this direction and you'll discover your true self.'

There are so many spiritual ideas and concepts around that help distract us from the experience of being human. Yet those distractions, as compelling as they seem, can imprison us in a pseudo-spiritual search for a freedom in which we already live.

You don't need to look in any direction to feel good. You don't need to know who you are, what you are, from where you came, where you're going, where is spiritual home, that you're love, the universe, God, oneness or one, a spiritual being having a human experience, not your thoughts or ego, that you're consciousness, or the all being, stardust or moon shadow.

You don't need to know anything.

You need not listen to other people's ideas and concepts of where to look, ideas that once you discover who you are you will also find some kind of knowing that brings peace and love.

That's just yet another idea, one that many chase.

You can NEVER know who you are, and anyone suggesting you look in this direction is suggesting you look for something that cannot be found.

At best, you may discover a feeling, a very nice one too, something that looks beyond all feelings you had before, something beyond words, a feeling of home, a knowing, the poetry of Love.

It's like Kool-Aid or spiritual cocaine. And once I've had my hit I'm going to preach and sell it to you too...

But you won't have found you or who you are. The suggestion that you will is one of the greatest hoodwinks ever. It's fooled most of even the most redeemed spiritual teachers, and simply encourages people to look for a reason to feel freedom and peace.

'Now I get a sense of x' (who I am) 'I feel y' (peace, love, freedom.

Now I have a deep and meaningful reason to feel something.

What if you relinquish this quest to know who you are? What if you don't need to know? What if peace, love, freedom, connection, unity, trust, creativity, and any other sales benefit listed in discovering who you are, are available to you right now without you needing to find, discover or understand anything?

What if there's absolutely no need to discover anything to feel happy? And furthermore, what if it's completely okay to not feel happy? What if it's completely okay to not have a clue about anything? What if we won't find out who we are, who or what God, or love is until some indeterminate time later, maybe after this lifetime? Maybe never.

What if it really doesn't matter and these are all just nice ideas?

What if all this searching, looking in a direction and preaching is distracting you from the one single thing you are here to do - life your life as a fallible, emotional-farting human being. Perhaps one who is not constantly trying to get in touch with whatever you are beyond that humanness?

What if you're here to live life without knowing and understanding?

What if you're here to feel good and bad, happy and sad, separate and 'one', lost and found, confused and clear, peace and anger, zen and, er, whatever is the opposite of zen, (which apparently is also zen...)?

Namaste Bitch!

What if you can feel all of that stuff without it meaning anything at all about who you truly are, without any of it being an invitation to embark on an endless quest for some kind of understanding?

What if it really doesn't matter who or what you are, you're just here to live and have all the experiences that life offers you?

What if you were not afraid of your experiences, and then, sometimes you were?

What if, instead of your quest for discovery of who or what you are and your searching and striving for a feeling, you were simply human, having very little clue about anything, had no idea who or what you are, and it just doesn't matter?

That looks like true freedom to me.

*Our expectations are often exposed to us, by not being met, in the most wonderful ways...*

# A Kind Reconnecting

I've reconnected with my Dad a couple of years ago in a way I never thought I would. For many years I held a grievance, even telling myself I had forgiven when I was still keeping out the connection that has been allowed to develop over the last couple of years.

We are very, very different! His idea of parenting laced with Victorian ideas from his own father, so different from my own progressive 21st century ideas.

Yet, holding on to any grievance only prolongs our suffering. We are essentially holding on to a misunderstanding. Yes, of course, we will always disagree with things people have said and done, but we need not hold on to the poison of grievance that keeps us from understanding and connection.

We need not hold on to our perceived knowing.

Once I allowed my own opinions about being right to subside, once I saw those opinions for what they were, I was able to hear my Dad and allow in a loving understanding of his very different point of view. I don't have to agree with it, but I now completely understand how that alternative point of view has come about, and the innocence of it. The desire of all Dads to do what they think is best, irrespective of whether, in the wisdom of hindsight and parental progression, it actually is.

If you're holding on to some kind of grievance about your Dad, indeed about anyone, I invite you to loosen your grip onto being right just a little, just enough to allow in a new way of seeing. Just enough to allow some light to shine on a new understanding, to allow love. Just enough to be kind.

You won't have to agree, you won't have to give up your own opinion, you won't even have to like someone. But your suffering from holding on to that grievance will almost certainly subside, and your experience of life will become a little more pleasant, lighter from letting go of the heaviness of carrying that bag of injustice.

Letting go of your grievance to allow some understanding is the kindest thing you can do, not just for your Dad, but moreover, for you.

And life really is too short to hold on to being right over being kind.

# Riding With Resilience

Several years ago I had a pretty fast motorcycle. A Suzuki Bandit 1200. I'd had half a dozen others previous to this one, but this was by far the quickest bike I'd ever owned. Really, stupidly fast, unnecessarily fast. Quick as...!!.

It was both thrilling and damn scary to ride!

I was never a 'once a biker, always a biker' guy. I wasn't into them at all until my late teens, then had a few years off them, but around age thirty got the bug again.

And maybe because it was never in my blood, it was quite easy to give up.

In the few years before I sold that last bike I started to hear of people I knew having mishaps. Friends of friends losing limbs, a death here and there of someone I'd heard of, then the most shocking: the death of a twin son of a very dear friend of the family. A life cut short so suddenly.

That was it! My yearly bike mileage had already reduced significantly, the enjoyment contaminated by thoughts of all those mishaps. But that young boy, way too close to home. As a family we loved their family.

After hearing of that tragedy I don't think I rode that bike again, a buyer collected it from my house.

After the accident our families drifted apart and lost contact with each other, through relocations and life taking different directions, and I've often thought about that lad's twin brother. I can't imagine the pain he must have felt at losing his twin. Did he feel like half of him was missing? Did the death of his brother also kill his desire to ride? How do you cope with that?

Well, one day a couple of years ago I saw him, for the first time since, now a fully grown man. I didn't get to speak to him, I didn't want to disturb him, he was sitting with a young lady having a drink and some crisps.

What struck me was he was sitting at that table, with that young lady, and two crash helmets. And close by, a very very fast motorcycle.

Obviously I have absolutely no idea how he feels or sees life, what he struggles with. But something in seeing him, with that lady, with that motorcycle, was soothing.

Whatever he had going on, whatever thoughts and memories visit him, there he was, doing something very ordinary, sitting outside a pub, by the sea, with a young lady, chatting and laughing away. And they'd obviously arrived by motorcycle.

Another example of the incredible resilience we have as human beings. Serendipitously, I'd noticed my own desire to get back on a bike a few days before seeing that young man. To experience that thrill and freedom, it really is like nothing else.

I'm sure he misses his brother. Maybe they are both riding on.

# There's a Lie in All BeLIEfs

I caught myself believing England can win the World Cup…

I started my exploration of personal development and study of human behaviour over twenty years ago, in 1998, and came across the understanding described by Syd Banks as The Three Principles in 2003 (although the label of 3Ps came later.) Looking back, since then I can see how I have entertained various beliefs, many of which have totally contradicted each other.

Like many others, I've also gone through the whole evangelical stage of 'seeing' something and believing it to be the ONLY thing we need to know

I have seen 'we are all one,' 'we are all love,' 'none of us exist,' yada yada yada… a whole bunch of other stuff too.

But then, I've also seen big monsters growing out of my walls coming to attack me…

I've seen the beauty of the heavens in the sky, wondered if I am there already, and contemplated hitting the ground off the top of tall buildings, like a watermelon. I've seen the nature of all that personal thinking, and have, too, felt like I have touched something beyond the energy of Thought.

Many times. For many years.

Over the last twenty two years I've had many beliefs, and over the last few years I've held on to very few of them.

Understanding the nature of beliefs, including 'we are not separate' and 'Romeo & Juliet by Dire Straits is the greatest love song ever,' has, in effect, liberated me from behaving in an evangelical 'come join my cult and have the same beliefs as us' way of suggesting anyone else should or will at some point see things the same as me.

It seems to me that comments like 'We are xyz, you'll see it one day' are about as presumptuous as anyone can get. Preaching a way of seeing the world, and suggesting other views have you be less loving or human has been the basis for all religious wars.

Whatever your beliefs, your proliferation of them as truth above all others can never be an agent for unity, only division, albeit you may pick up some disciples along the way.

Really understanding the nature of the human experience, the nature of beliefs, really seeing how made up even our most compelling, deeply 'held' beliefs and ways of seeing are, that just may help us all live together in harmony.

A very simple understanding and embracing of the nature of our experience and differences, without needing to replace one conceptual idea with another.

Although Romeo & Juliet by Dire Straits really is the greatest love song ever, and this really IS the only Truth you need to know. Give it a listen, you'll feel it too one day...

At least that's how it looks to me.
Today.

After twenty two years.

In twenty minutes, who knows...

Come on England!

# The Subtle Trap of Ideas

"Oh I know, Phil, I know... "

He spoke with such beautiful empathy, a love and compassion so full it left no room for doubt. He did know, and on hearing his next few words, every possibility, including the end of my suffering, tore open for me.

***"Even your most noble beliefs about love have you suffer."***

As I allowed myself to consider what I just heard, what I was being shown, I felt my suffering dissolve. A mix of bittersweet relief washed through me, it's sweetness tainted by an egoic sadness as I watched my romantic ideas about love being revealed for what they were - just ideas.

I could see so clearly that for every idea I held onto, for every belief, there would always be a different, contradictory and often paradoxical view, and that whenever I defined anything, any thing, by way of a belief or idea, in my defining was a confining. And by definition, confining was an act of imprisonment against the freedom of the undefined.

The more I held on to any idea, be it a noble idea about love, how things are or should be, the more I would feel resistance when presented with any contradictory views outside of that idea.

I've seen this in other communities, too. Some of the most aggressive and defensive behaviour I've witnessed on social media coming from those preaching a particular and perhaps noble idea about love and Truth with a capital 'T.'

Yet as we recognise our ideas and beliefs as just another transient manifestation of the energy of life, the energy of thought, it seems to me that even the solid lines of our most compelling beliefs soften into a liberating unknown.

Ah, the beauty and freedom of the unknown. Acknowledging but not being directed by my egotistic desire to be right, to know my true self, to know 'Truth', noticing the egotistic desire to simply know.

I have many ideas, entertain many beliefs, and am torn open to the infinite possibility that each and every one of them may be myth. My ideas and beliefs have become a reminder that I don't know, a reminder of being caught in the illusion of knowing, and the suffering that any belief can bring.

If we think that any discovery or belief about truth, love, or who we are is what brings us peace then we don't understand the real source of peace.

And now when I see people touting 'Truth' and the like, ideas and understandings that bring peace, I find myself whispering "Oh, I know... I know..." and am myself filled with compassion.

Freedom, love and compassion.

Love... Now that IS my favourite idea...

*'...and then I remembered love.'*

# What Do You Want?

What do you want?

'I don't know.'

I've asked this question a thousand times and heard that answer almost as many.

In most cases 'I don't know' is simply code for 'I know what I want but I don't believe I can have it.' Or the alternative - 'I feel too much shame, embarrassment, a lack of self-worth, some other derogatory feeling about myself to admit and own what I want.'

Yet time and time again I see with my clients, and indeed in my own life, that when we simply get clear and honest about what we want, without entertaining all the additional noise around it, life seems to conspire to provide us with it.

I've seen it with relationships, jobs, promotions and other career opportunities, clients, business growth, health, holidays and travel, and all manner of stuff that is available for us to experience in this life.

All the time we entertain the plethora of dismissive excuses and disbeliefs - 'She's out of my league,' 'they'll never pay that much,' 'he'd never do that,' 'I don't deserve that,' or 'I just don't think it's possible,' - we seem to drown out the possibility of even seeing opportunities to get closer to what we really want.

This whole saga reminds me of one of my favourite quotes by William Hutchison Murray:

*"Until one is committed, there is hesitancy, the chance to draw back, always ineffectiveness. Concerning all acts of initiative (and creation), there is one elementary truth, the ignorance of which kills countless ideas and splendid plans: that the moment one definitely commits oneself, then Providence moves too. All sorts of things occur to help one that would never otherwise have occurred. A whole stream of events issues from the decision, raising in one's favour all manner of unforeseen incidents and meetings and material assistance, which no man could have dreamt would have come his way. I have learned a deep respect for one of Goethe's couplets:*

*Whatever you can do, or dream you can, begin it.*

*Boldness has genius, power, and magic in it!"*

Surely that first step of commitment of which Murray refers is being honest and owning what we want. Not tentatively, but without the constant excuses and dismissals, by simply and honestly owning 'I want this.' Period. Full stop.

I want. No story.

Having absolutely no idea how whatever that is may come to fruition can, as far as I can tell, be part of the fun of welcoming whatever you want into your life. 'Come on, show me, guide me, show me where you're at!' Inviting it in, instead of dismissing it with a no-entry sign at the door.

And of course, what we want may show up in ways completely unfamiliar or unexpected, and on the face of it may look nothing like we've imagined. But we can only find this out if we are willing to explore, not through the eyes of fears, assumption and prediction, or through the eyes of apparent knowing, but through the eyes of possibility and not knowing.

I've seen clients mysteriously meet life partners, gain promotions and new jobs, work with dream clients, make dream house-moves and relocations, create wealth, and experience new levels of happiness and intimacy. (These last two are my favourites!). But only once they've got honest. 'Yes, I do want that.'

I've got jobs and promotions, created packages and events and charged fees, bought cars & houses, travelled, built lifestyles and even dated in ways that the noise in my head had said was not possible.

What does that noise in my head know anyway? On reflection, very little! Especially when it is the jabbering noise of fear and cynicism.

Any cynicism is simply a reflection of the extent to which we hold on to past disappointments.

Expect to be disappointed, get disappointed.

So much magic seems to be available to us when we let that shit go. Let shit go.

Flush and get back to the dance floor of life, expecting to be pleasantly surprised in unknown and wonderful ways, and you'll likely be just that. And have fun dancing. Joy seems to be an agent for miracles, yet cynicism, dishonesty and fear kill joy.

What do you want, irrespective of any noise you have going on about having it? Not what do you want as secondary because you don't believe what you really want actually exists or is attainable. Not the 'nice place to live with lots of stuff' because 'an intimate relationship with someone in which where we live becomes irrelevant' is not possible.

What do you honestly want, without that cynicism or fear? Are you willing to gift yourself that level of honesty with yourself? To date your desires, lovingly, unconditionally, without them meaning anything about you or their possibility?

What if you committed to the intimacy of that honesty, without judgment? Allowed yourself to just dance in the joy of being honest with yourself about your desires.

Then watch what happens...

# What Would Love Do?

It almost always amuses me when a friend reflects aspects of my own work back at me.

There I am, all caught up in a story of betrayal, occasionally stepping out of it to watch it unfold, and this is said.

'Oh, you are still angry, aren't you? What would love do?'

Haha! Maybe my all time favourite question, ever!

Most times, (but of course not always,) the simple act of asking this question helps any anger dissolve, reminds us that whatever the situation, there is love and understanding available, and often provides a small glint of light on a pathway to wisdom, to being guided by kindness and compassion, to others and to ourselves.

Actions taken from anger or hurt, fearful actions (anger is always fear based,) rarely, if ever improve matters.

Personally, this question almost always reminds me that there's nothing to even forgive, that everyone only ever behaves in one of two ways - a call for love or an expression of love - and that anger is only my ego telling me something should be different to how it is. Most often it's telling me someone should have behaved differently to how they behaved…

Connecting with love and compassion reminds me we're all only ever acting out of what we believe in the moment, the very transient moment, and that many of us frequently feel disconnected from love and lost in a fearful view of the world. As far as I can tell, it's called being human.

And it still feels important to me to honour the values that feel true for me, or simply that I hold dear irrespective of any truth, such as honesty, integrity and kindness, and I get to choose, also in each moment, the extent to which my compassion for others allows them to play out in my life.

When I am caught up in my own fears and anger, it becomes very difficult to connect with the self-love that is at the heart of our ability to show kindness and compassion to others.

So maybe love is simply at the heart of our human experience. The dance between being energised by love, or under an illusion of separation from love.

'What would love do?' helps me remember that too.

# All Natural

You can never have a feeling or emotion you are not meant to have. You are part of nature, this magical, mystical, perfect system that encompasses us all, the living and breathing of life. Whatever you feel, however life looks to you, ecstatic in bliss or the despair of heartbreak, in deep peace or raging in anger, laughing or crying, lost or grounded, you are always an expression of nature.

A rose that blooms or withers, all natural.

Your true nature is not something to be discovered, it is, always has been, always will be, exactly as you are in any moment.

Aware or unaware. Natural. There is nothing for you to do or be to find who you truly are, those quests just have you delve deeper into another story and concept about you.

You are you, however that is expressing.

Nature. Natural.

Now.

# We Need No Understanding to Feel Peace

Equally, we need no understanding to feel love.

Every day we see people proliferating ideas about what brings peace. The suggestions are often very subtle - some version of 'once you see this you'll feel that.'

The moment someone suggests that when you understand x you'll feel y, they are simply suggesting you replace one conceptual idea with another, one made-up dependency for peace with another.

Yet peace has no dependencies and requires no explanation or understanding. It is story-less, despite your story.

The shift from 'when I have a billion quid / can make a chocolate cake that rises / lose 20 pounds / get through a day without wanting someone else to change' to 'we are all one / you only need know your true self / consciousness is having a fun party experimenting with hallucinogenic drugs aka humans' is not necessary to experience your innate capability to feel any emotion, including peace, love and compassion.

Sure, many of these ideas feel true, seem to invoke some kind of nice feeling in most of us, inspire poetry and a sense of connection to something greater than ourselves. By all means explore and play with these nice ideas, especially if it's fun and feels good. But that's all they are. Nice ideas that often feel true.

No one knows.

Peace is not in pretending to know. Of course, us humans like to know stuff, we want to understand, so when we entertain an idea that feels true and gives a reason for peace, it makes sense that it feels good. We might even feel like we're home, get a glimpse of our true self or God, such is the perceived security of 'knowing.'

Yet, peace has no dependencies at all. Least of all understandings for which humans have searched for millennia.

And if you disagree with me here, that's okay too. It doesn't matter. Peace is available to you, regardless of whether we agree or not.

You don't need to understand or know anything to feel peace, to feel love, despite all of life's noise to the contrary, including noise portrayed as the only understanding you need.

Peace is free.

Free of all understanding, concepts and ideas. About us, the world, God, consciousness, fruit cake and bananas.

Maybe peace is just another name for love.

Or maybe that's just another nice idea too...

*Neither true friendship nor true love need be chased. Both will accompany you wherever you are.*

# Together We Rise

A.k.a. - Don't dis my accountability...

I don't know about you, but I pretty much ALWAYS do what I say I'm going to do...

...if it has an impact on someone else.

Even if that impact is the simple act of telling someone I'm going to do it. Like all of us, I have many ideas about myself, and one of my favourite ones is my integrity - when I say I will do something, I damn well do it!

Because underneath all the stories of enlightenment, I do care what you think about me, and also because of the somewhat stubborn nature of my personality, telling you I'll do something seems to provide me with a kind of self-image-preserving motivation to get things done.

See! I told you I'd do it! Impressed? Cue feeling good about myself...

In any case, whatever the psychological reasoning, sharing my intentions motivates my accountability.

Alas, I also notice that is not always the case when the only person I've told is me...

Is this some deep lack of commitment on my part? Do I have some commitment issues or commitment phobia? Am I a master procrastinator or some other 'I am broken' label? Do I need to do a shed load more work on myself, perhaps go do some deep work with a master coach for the price of a small house?

I doubt it...

After studying human behaviour and the nature of our experience of life for over twenty years, it looks much simpler to me.

Alone, we are much more prone to allowing our stories to direct our action. Alone, when our lack of action has no effect on others, most of us are much more prone to inaction.

Yes, of course it is absolutely useful and helpful to discover our deeper 'why' and be in touch with our heart's desires, to help us move from inaction into action. They are all forms of motivation.

And still, with some things, I notice if we are not held accountable we are simply less likely to move, to act.

This is why working with a personal trainer works, and why most of us make more effort to keep an appointment with someone else than providing ourselves with some 'me time'.

Maybe you're different. That's cool. Or maybe your perceived difference is just an idea, and you, like me, also exhibit this natural human phenomenon.

Many coaches claim to not play the role of 'accountability coach' yet the mere act of having you commit to do something, even declare your intention on a call, does provide some level of accountability.

So let's be up front about this whole accountability thing. As a coach I WILL hold you accountable to what you want. Because I know it will help you get what you want. Period.

Sure, we'll continue to explore your deeper desires and the role you allow your stories to play in your life, and accountability may diminish into an irrelevance as you come to see and own your deeper desires, as you develop the discipline of remembering what you want.

Indeed it is the remembering of what you want that brings the discipline of taking action towards it.

Discipline is simply remembering what you want. Without being distracted by any other stories.

And in the meantime...

Without doubt accountability does help us take action, and it's only action that has us create what we want in the world.

Accountability coach?

Who cares?

I'll just do whatever I feel helps you.

Irrespective of stories. Irrespective of rules.

Because I want you to have what you want, I'll hold you accountable to what you want.

Would you like to be held accountable to that too?

# The Moment Sucks

*'I know I should live in the moment but the moment fucking sucks!'*

One of my most favourite things a client has ever said.

And there's something in this. Sometimes the present moment does suck!

We see lots of stuff about how living and being present to the moment is the way to end all suffering, (along with remembering who we are, and we are all one, which I guess means there is only ever one moment too... jeez I hope the sickness isn't everlastin...)

Anyways...

I see sometimes the current moment does, indeed, fucking suck!

Like it did a few days ago:

I went to the dentist, for a regular check-up, the dentist did that whole cleaning and scraping thing. Oh, how lovely to be able to feel, once again, the space between my teeth, but the process itself is chuffing painful! Sorry, maybe this is a Man-Card revocation, but hands-up who actually enjoys having their teeth cleaned? Right! No one! Not even Rambo!

Those moments suck!

In fact, being really present to the moment, the scraping, the prodding, the blood, the more I focused on what was actually happening in that moment the more it chuffing hurt!

Like - oh just focus on the pain, it will help!

Fact is, sometimes the moment does suck! Which also highlights the fallacy of all these mantras and 'rules to live by' that we see proliferated around.

There is no single and simple way to live. If there were, don't you think someone would have written a book about it by now, it would have been a runaway success, and all those other books in the personal development section at Barnes & Noble or Waterstones would disappear into oblivion....

Even living in the moment is not always the most helpful thing to do.

Whilst the dentist was cleaning and scraping my teeth, (and gums, FFS!) I actually counted my breaths, knowing that the last time I did that it was all over before I got to breath number two-hundred. Well before that. So my strategy for handling that uncomfortable situation, for handling the moment that sucked, was to remember and imagine that the moment would be over soon. It was to remember that there was a future beyond the current moment.

Live in the moment? Yeah... sometimes....

There are no rules. When we define we confine. We limit the infinite freedom of life.

So, when anyone suggests to you to live in the moment, that is just that, a suggestion.

Without doing harm to yourself or others, I suggest just doing whatever helps.

Since our experience of life is only ever created through the energy of thought, and the manifestation of those thoughts are infinitely variable, in size, shape, colour, and smell, there really can never be a single strategy for you to 'suffer less.'

We can only ever do what helps 'in the moment.'

Aha yes, the moment....

Imagine a future, remember a past, drop everything and get present. Yeah, those are all options.

The closer I look at this the more I'm convinced it's not even possible to completely live in the moment, because we always bring some distant memory of a past and some imagination, some hope and fear, about the future.

Live in the moment?

Yeah, in this moment imagine whatever helps...

That might be imagining some future event, perhaps sitting on a beautiful beach with a Mojito whilst your dentist picks thorns out of his ass....

Just do whatever works.

No rules.

# Being at One

None of us can ever be free of the limitations of our consciousness unless we're able to, and indeed willing, to go beyond all concepts.

Rather than embracing even our most loving and spiritual beliefs, even our most heart-felt or compelling ideas of who we are or what we are, our freedom lies in seeing all of them, in seeing all these ideas, concepts and beliefs only ever as perceptions of truth.

If there is freedom, in itself also a concept, it is surely beyond even the ideas we have of it, and certainly beyond any ideas we have of ourselves.

Beyond even the ideas we have of love.

*It's been so liberating to realise that even when I think I'm right, I actually might not be.*

# My Promise

*"I promise to only speak to the person I see. That might not be the person you think I should see."*

I share this promise the first time I have a conversation with someone. It's often not until much later that they really get what I mean.

We're so often taught that we are the sum total of our experiences in life, and the average of the people around us. For many this can mean that we are a product of the trauma and abuse we have experienced, or have become defined in some way by being around our abusers.

Yet there is an undefined and undefinable essence to us with which we arrived here, and has always been in us. It is the part of us that is ever-present and in all of us, despite the hundreds and thousands of stories told to us and the many more we tell ourselves.

The truth is, we are not our past, our past experiences or our past behaviour. We are not even our present behaviour. Whilst we form an identity of ourselves through our experiences, our identity is only ever an image of how we see ourselves, and is only ever a product of an intellect whose sole quest is to understand 'who am I?'

Identity is only ever an image of a past that is no longer real. All identities are, therefore, illusionary and imagined. Sure, some teach the power of creating an identity of who you want to be, now or in the future. That, too, only exists as an illusionary association with thoughts of the future that have immediately passed.

Whatever your past experiences, however you have previously seen yourself, however strongly you may feel associated with your past and the walls created in it, the you that arrived here is still within you. Your unconditioned self is still 'within' you, one that cannot be contaminated by made up meanings from any and all of your experiences.

So much of our lives is outwardly focused; on what's going on around us, on our experiences and behaviours, on creating memories that we can add to our self-image and identity. This can make remembering the undefinable freedom of who we are at our core, remembering our unconditioned self, feel like trying to remember the first picture we saw as a baby. Too distant, though all of life already lived, to connect with.

So much noise obscuring the view of who we are.

Your self-image will never believe how beautiful your soul is. The judgment that is the sole nature of your self-image cannot even grasp the beauty of you and the essence of love.

But that doesn't mean it's not there. You may have people in your life who see it in you. Be with them. Allow your heart to open to them, and allow yourself to see it in them too. As you see beyond people's pasts and beyond their experiences, beyond their identity of the abused or even the abuser, so too shall they see you.

And in opening your heart to them you just might remember more of who you are. Undefined and free.

# You Are a Banana

You are a banana. Don't you feel better now?

It's a subtle yet prolific hypnosis. When you see this you'll feel that.

When you understand how life works, you'll feel more peace.

When you see we are all one, or not separate, you'll no longer be desperate to defend or feel secure.

When you love yourself, you'll experience a more loving life. (It took me a quite some time to see past this one!)

When you look in this direction, be it within or towards some other idea, you'll FEEL something, basically more nice stuff...

Here's how it looks to me:

I don't need to do, see, understand or look in any direction to feel anything. I can associate a feeling of profound peace without 'looking within,' also known as 'thinking particular thoughts,' or the illusion of 'no thoughts.'

Sure, those of us working in this field will have observed people's experiences as they explore different understandings, concepts and ideas. We might even observe some trends. Yet even some of the 'spiritual teachers' of these hypnotic understandings will tell you that unless it's true all the time, it's not true at all. Or maybe that it might not be true, but they'll teach until it's proven false.

I talk with people who have explored various understandings of this nature, yet haven't fallen under the hypnotic spell, and they often ask a version of 'I get it, but I'm not feeling it. What the hell is wrong with me?' In a cult-like manner, if you don't have the predicted outcome in your life from understanding these ideas, concepts or principles, it might be suggested that you simply don't get it, such is the strength of conviction of predicting others experience and behaviours in some communities. Much to my amusement I've had it suggested to me 'Don't worry, you'll get there,' something that genuinely had me laugh out loud. Get where exactly? Oh, under the spell of an alternative concept...

Perhaps when we 'get it' that peace is free, there is nowhere to 'get to.' And of course it's still fun to explore and go on 'road trips and rides'...

Hey, we're all just doing what makes sense to us, and of course when we come across a concept or idea that doesn't look like a concept or idea, an 'understanding' that seems to, in and of itself, bring a more peaceful and loving life, who wouldn't want more of that?

Who doesn't want to play better, have more joy, feel more love? And if I can present some 'thing' to you that looks like it will help you have that, I'll look like I'm onto something. Even if that 'thing' is an understanding. An understand-thing.

Compelling indeed.

Yet, have you noticed how the energy of 'Aha, now I understand' is ohhhh so similar to 'Aha, there's nothing to understand'? Give it a go. Play with that and see how it feels.

Here's the contradiction in my post. When you understand you don't need to understand, it looks to me like you may also feel peace. But only sometimes. And really, what I'm saying is, peace is available to you freely, irrespective of any concept, idea or understanding. Without any thing, any understand-thing.

So if you've been exploring some new ideas, concepts or principles, and you're not having any of the predicted experiences of some teachers and coaches, that also makes complete sense, given the nature of how our experience of life seems to work. Given how feelings of peace, love and freedom arise - freely, without attachment to any-thing.

So that banana 'thing.' Did you know that, in a certain context, you are made of exactly the same stuff as a banana? There is scientific evidence to prove this fact, and apparently knowing you are the same as everyone and everything in this universe can bring you peace.

So now you can consider this and be hypnotised by the idea of a banana...

Free peace and love to you, whatever you feel, teach, say, do, comment, like or understand.

# We All Do It

On my regular walk around Tsilivi, on the Greek island of Zakynthos, I often sneak into one particular hotel (sneak, as in walk in, head held high as if I own the place) to, ummm, well, do what one needs to do.

I've only actually stayed at this hotel once, way back in 2001 on my first ever trip there. And almost every time I'm about to walk in, I imagine a challenging conversation, someone asking me if I'm a guest, and me explaining that I have been, once upon a time. And of course, no one ever bats an eyelid...

On one particular visit, (I'll spare you the details but it was only a brief standing visit,) I had a thought:

Everyone one of us poops.

Okay, now this fact may not seem like news to you, it wasn't really news to me, but it highlights something that seems important and useful to remember.

Thankfully, and with the exception of only one of my friends, none of us shares many details of our pooping. I am particularly grateful my social media is not flush with such pictures and posts... That's my personal preference, and I'll bet it's a common one.

However, whilst we all poop, we also all get on a downer occasionally. I've never met anyone who didn't have sad thoughts, anxious thoughts, to varying degrees depressive moods, low moods, feeling like a total loser moods, as well as the blissfully happy moods about which we are willing to share.

And for the most part we treat these downers as drowners, like poop, and keep them to ourselves.

Well, I want to remind you that at times WE ALL have shit going on, we all occasionally feel like shit, and life looks shit. And whilst this isn't an invitation to share, it's not an invitation to continue hiding either. I just want you to know that, just like pooping, EVERY SINGLE ONE OF US experiences a whole range of emotions and perspectives on life. Even the most omming of spiritual teachers I know is fundamentally human.

Just because there are no poop pics, doesn't mean it's not going on.

You are definitely not alone, and it's okay. In fact it's more than okay. It's really not wise to try to resist the pooping, or resist how you feel.

We really don't need to hide our humanness from others, or pretend it doesn't happen. Indeed it's my experience that people connect most deeply to the humanness we so often try to hide. Anyone who's had a prolonged stay in a hospital will know the camaraderie, connection and compassion that comes from the unavoidable sharing of what it is to be human.

We are loved because we are human, not despite of it.

The thought of this whole analogy between pooping and low moods had me chuckle, as did the subsequent thought about me sneaking into hotels to use their bathrooms to pee...

Maybe I'll share more of my humanness too. Maybe I'll start a new movement (see what I did there?) and create an Instagram page of pictures from bathrooms where I go to pee for free.

The Free Pees.

Keep walking. Keep smiling. Keep loving.

Stay regular

# The Story of You

When I'm coaching someone, I always want to allow myself to be connected to them, which means really listening to the story they have of themselves.

And at the same time, in service to my client, I do not want to either succumb to or add to that story. At first this might seem to present a fascinating dichotomy; how can I truly connect with the story but not succumb to it?

Yet in essence, it's very simple.

I know with all my being the person in front of me is not their story. So whatever they share with me is just telling me and enabling me to get an understanding of how they see, and more empowering, how they are looking at the world.

My basis for connection is in knowing the possibilities for the person irrespective of, and beyond their stories. And this enables me to connect with just about anyone. When I'm asking 'So what's going on with you?' I am actually asking 'So, what stories are you telling yourself right now?'

Given that we experience all of life through the stories we tell ourselves about it, I often have great compassion for people and the limitations through which they look at life and the world. We all do it to varying degrees. My compassion comes from knowing this is all part of the human experience, story after story after story.

Some might be tempted to start to delve into those stories, I occasionally catch myself too. Sometimes it's subtle, offering a counterargument to how the story is untrue. But I'm of most service to my client when I am able to help them see that all of what they are experiencing is story, irrespective of its content.

I notice, and indeed recognise in myself the persistent predictions and reflections. 'Oh I hear you. Me too. That's oh so similar to a shit movie I used to make up about myself and watch over and over.'

There's a shift available to all of us, that of allowing life to show us new stories. Okay, maybe slightly more correctly, that of allowing life to show us opportunities for us to create new stories.

I might not enjoy the movie I'm about to go see, but I won't know until I go watch it. And hey, it's okay to go to a movie and not enjoy it. To think we should enjoy everything is just yet another story.

The more I become aware of the nature, rather than the content, of the stories I persistently tell myself, the more I've personally noticed I'm also open to seeing something different, seeing something new. Your mileage may vary, but I'd guess something similar may happen for you too.

Byron Katie sums it up beautifully with her question - Who would you be without your story?

Free. The answer is always free.

# Living

Love.

Fall.

Fail.

Want.

Obsess.

Resist.

You cannot quell the flow of life.

You're here to love, to fall, to fail, to want, to obsess.

Even to resist.

It's okay to feel attached - to love, to someone, to an idea, to a dream.

Life loves you and flows independent of your delusions.

You are here to fall in love, to want, to attach and resist,

To cry in the arms of broken dreams and dance in the joy of desires met.

Your work is not to find ways to avoid and overcome experiences,

But to allow yourself to be immersed in them.

Life is here to be lived.

Live it.

*There is no feeling you desire that you do not already have the ability to feel.*

# I Love You

I notice occasions when I don't want to say those three little words - I Love you - despite all that I teach and coach around.

Someone may say it in a comment on social media, 'I love you, Phil!' and I have some reluctance to respond in the same way, instead opting for some other safer version:

'Love you too, brother' just so you're sure this is a brotherly love thing...

'Loving you' which some suggest is more accurate to what we 'do' but for me still doesn't feel as intimate as the simple 'I love you.'

'Much love' and 'sending you loads of love' are my most common half-arsed cop-outs from simple human intimacy.

If someone asks me to sign a book, (which always amuses me anyway,) I'll often sign 'love always'. I like this, it has so many meanings...

To some of my close friends, maybe an 'I love yoouuuuuu!' just to string it out and add some distracting humour.

Any of this sound familiar to you?

I don't have this reluctance going on all the time, of course, it may be there's some 'romantic love' interest thing going on, I want to avoid confusion, or just generally listening to some other insecurity. But always, ALWAYS, in some way distracted from the purity and simplicity of love.

There are times when I don't take any notice at all of any of that thinking, and I'm throwing this 'I love you' thing around like glitter at a unicorn party.

Catching this reluctance reminds me to slow down and take a look at what's going on. Discomfort is great for that - reminding me I am believing something that is unlikely to be true. Reminding me I am overthinking, creating unnecessary meaning and entertaining fears.

There are few sentences as simple and true as 'I love you.' It is only ever our insecurities and confusion that have us either withhold it, or add more meaning to it. And when we strip away all that noise, love is always there, every time, between everyone.

It looks to me that us humans are excellent at loving each other, just a bit crap at expressing it, or indeed confusing it with something else.

So just for clarity, if you're reading this, I love you.

I can't not do that, despite what my fears try and tell me.

*Love more*
*Judge Less*

# H2O - The Water of Life

**H**onesty - Only sharing what seems like truth, never any intent to deceive or withhold truth. Connecting with and being open to love, admitting and being open with fear. Being honest with my experiences of life.

**H**umour - A preference for seeing the lighter side of life, not taking life and circumstances too seriously. Seeing life as a sitcom rather than a documentary, bringing joy, spreading smiles. Often teasing, rarely serious, always sincere.

**O**penness - Open to adventure, to learning, to intimacy. Open to sharing and showing all of me, and open to seeing things differently. Holding lightly current views and beliefs, knowing that any may become myth tomorrow. Open to allowing the flow of nature, of life, and the new.

Life, living with honesty, humour and openness.

Living with love

# Leading to Love with Love

How does Love lead to more Love?

In opening up to a more loving world, in the beautiful uncontaminated space of that exploration, last night I suddenly remembered a story my Dad used to read to me at night when I was a very small boy. The contents of the memory were sweet, but it was the existence of the memory itself that touched me.

For much of my life I'd told myself some quite unpleasant stories about my Dad. Many self-righteous stories of how he should have behaved differently keeping at bay glimpses of love he had shown. Sweeter memories, apparently always available, buried deeply beneath my self-proliferating stories of victimhood.

Last night, out of the affection in the conversation, the memory of my Dad sitting on the edge of my bed, reading this particular story - The Whispering Rabbit - came home to me, and with much delight I also remembered I still have the book. This discovery had me wondering just how many of these moments in my childhood history are available for me to recall and love now?

And in that loving inquiry, others arrived: His taking me out, just the two of us, when I was a heartbroken young teenager; having coffee with cheese & crackers prepared by my Mum, as I helped him with some DIY project in our house; Gifts he claimed 'fell off the back of a lorry' that I later found out he had actually purchased for me...

I could choose some version of an unhelpful story that there are not many such memories, but I know there are others and I am open to them also arriving.

In life there are rainy, stormy days, and bright, warm sunny days. Days filled with fun & laughter, times of bitter disappointment, anger and sadness. By the time we reach our early forties we've lived over fifteen thousand days in which to create many thousands of memories. I've noticed how much more pleasant my experience is of life when I choose to give energy to that which I find joyful and loving, rather than bitter and resentful. And in my understanding of love and how we experience life, resentment dissolves.

The more I am open to love, share love, allow love, the more I allow compassion, the more love life seems to show me. Of course I'm simply seeing and feeling more of what's been there all along, allowing it into my life without the filters of the stories of my past.

I'll bet each and every one of us has available to us some sweeter memories than we've allowed to show through our stories of just how chuffing hard life has been and can be.

Sweeter memories awaiting for us to let them in.

And I hope my remembering this one about my Dad and my reading this story created a memory just as sweet for someone else too.

*I can only feel insulted if I am defending an idea.*

# The Amusement of Who You Really Are

Twenty two years ago I started looking at human behaviour and how we experience life, wanting to understand what had brought me to that point in my own life and also motivated by wanting to understand what I could have done differently.

Of course, I've seen since that I could not have done anything differently, given the understanding I had at the time. It is understanding, and often misunderstanding, that is the biggest factor in determining any behaviour.

I stumbled across an insight on 2003 that changed how I saw how we experience everything in life, a 'dropped the book' moment, and have continued that exploration since, making it the foundation for all of my professional work since 2005.

Up until a couple of years ago, that foundation was centred around helping people understand love, the nature of our experience of life, and who they truly are. It appeared to me that understanding what is often called 'our true nature' was the key to the dissolution of everything that kept us from love, from peace, from intimacy, from success.

Indeed social media nowadays is filled with a plethora of people talking all about understanding who you are, the illusion of separation, and the non-dualistic nature of our very being.

And I also notice that life leaves clues.

Something that has fascinated me about the premise of understanding who we really are being the pathless path to peace is that I have experienced more animosity from some teachers in this area than any other on social media. A growing circle that now includes some friends, wanting to point out how wrong or unhelpful anything is that doesn't fit with their way of seeing.

That in and of itself looks like a big clue to me.

And given the insight I had a couple of years ago, it also now makes complete sense.

It's not possible to live in a belief-less world, just as it is not possible to live an egoless life. Only the ego would believe such a way is possible.

And to that end, only an ego would make claims to a true nature, a true self, indeed to any truth.

Of course it's not possible to describe the full impact of that insight in a single chapter in a book. It took me almost twenty years of exploration to get there, including an in-depth immersion in the 3Ps, non-duality teachings, so many other ideas and concepts and claims of truth, and a whole lifetime to prepare for it.

That insight has revealed a Free Peace that is independent of any idea, concept, understanding, or supposed truth, and has helped me see the amusement in so much of what else is out there and the manner in which it is shared. The amusement and humour, the love, the joy, the freedom of what it is to be human. All without any desire to curate, censor, delete, abuse, accuse, make wrong, or convince.

The Free Peace and joy of seeing it all.

It is that freedom, that liberation, that I will be continuing to explore with my clients in the future.

And my invitation to you is this:

If you have you been navigating a myriad of different philosophical, spiritual and personal development understandings, relentlessly searching for that one 'thing' that will have you feel entirely free to be you and live the life you want, with all its riches and liberation, pause and consider that perhaps it has been your searching that has distracted you from freedom and peace.

Similarly, if you have found that 'one thing', a single understanding, a single paradigm, 'the only thing anyone needs to know' that is the enabler for peace, freedom, living life to the full, I invite you to explore beyond those ideas, a peace without the dependency of any 'one thing'.

Peace irrelevant to oneness, a true self, true nature, non-duality, who you are, comments on social media, the blueprint specification of consciousness, or the misinterpreted words of any philosopher. Beyond any 'thing.'

The Free Peace.

# Stop Focusing On What You Want

## *And allow your self to die, instead.*

It goes like this:

Born, happy.

Then it's often inadvertently downhill...

We're taught that happiness comes from some societal norms, ideas of what makes for a good life and a happy person, but what we really learn is how to be unhappy when we are non-conformant. We become conditioned into believing that we must have certain things in certain ways in life to be happy, and we build an identity around that, developing who we think we are by spending life chasing all those things and circumstances, colours and shapes that we associate with happiness.

There are some subtle differences between cultures, some not so subtle, but for all of us what life should look like becomes the foundation for the image of who we think we are and need to be.

Along the way some people just settle, continuing to nurse a desire for 'more', entering the lottery, living in hope, deciding life isn't so bad being a little bit miserable.

Others invest in educating themselves on how to reach their goals, how to acquire and build the life they've learnt to want, using their remaining life energy for a relentless pursuit.

Life becomes the pursuit.

Since happiness, love, joy and peace can never come from the pursuit itself, there's an endless supply of books and programs teaching us different ways to achieve the unachievable. We can never get enough of what we don't really need.

And of course, if it's not working, it's either you're not doing it right, or you need a different book.

But what if our chasing these ideas of what we think we want to be happy and loved are exactly what keep us from happiness and love?

The oldest guy to come to me with this realisation was around seventy five. That's a lot of years to be chasing, pursuing & delaying happiness. That's a lot of effort in keeping out love.

Life already loves us. Only our ideas of how it should look keep us from experiencing all the love that is already here.

This plays out in a manner of ways. One client recently became open to his business going in a particular direction, something he had resisted previously and that seemed to bring some anxiety when the opportunity presented itself. Two months in he's loving all that is being created and what he is now bringing to his customers.

Just this morning yet another conversation with someone who is in awe at seeing how the dots have joined up to bring her where she is, in support of what is for her, despite her persistent resistance. And it relates to everything, including much about her job and where she lives.

And in talking with a friend about this yesterday I remembered a conversation I had with a client a little over a year ago. She'd said if I'd asked her a few years previous if she could imagine moving to the country where she now lives to be with the kind of man she now lives with, she'd have said 'no way, I don't want that.' Yet I remembered yesterday her saying she'd never swap the reality she has now for the dream she once had. That struck me at the time, how for many of us what we think we want can distract us from joys available now.

For her to embrace what life was offering she had to allow the death of who she thought she was going to be. That can come with all of the usual feelings grief brings - sadness, anxiety, even anger, same as any other loss. The death of a conditioned self and the idea of a life necessary to allow the embracing of the beautiful now.

Letting previous ideas of what life and love looks like die, to let love in now.

We're often at ease with allowing this for supposedly smaller things in life, but the really big things? Our big ideas? Wow, no way are we going to be letting go and letting God for those...

And whilst we hold on to conformity and our own expectations, resisting what is, life sometimes slaps us repeatedly to show who's in charge. And it isn't the little one with the big ideas...

The happiest people I know are not concerned with a societal conditioned conformity. Indeed they are not so concerned with chasing or maintaining a version of themselves. They are just happy. Rather than resist, they've embraced what is in front of them, what has been presented to them, there's an openness to receive rather than a desire to chase. They play and explore rather than pursue.

And whilst this might look out of alignment with us being honest with ourselves about what we want, there's a subtle and important piece that is taught in many circles yet is still missed.

Dr Wayne Dyer taught people to be in touch with the feelings as if their wishes had already been fulfilled, not to be concerned with the details of the wishes themselves. Many other teachers, such as Abraham Hicks and others around the law of attraction, suggest the same.

Because it is never the things or the circumstances we wish for that bring the feelings we want. Most who look back on life do so wishing they had allowed themselves to be happy with what is, allowed themselves to embrace what life was offering them beyond their ideas of life. Give up the relentless chasing and delaying of living in pursuit of wants in a conditioned dream.

To do that we must allow the chaser to die, the one who defines and therefore confines, the one who resists. Surrendering the details of our ideas that so often keep us from what is available to us right now in ways we simply cannot imagine.

Love, peace, joy, and happiness.

# A Dogmatic Desertion

Please don't tell me the only reason I suffer is because I have forgotten I am not separate from you, or that I have essentially forgotten God.

I suffer because I am experiencing being a beautiful human being. We suffer because we are alive, because we love, because we want, we dance, we live, we fall, we fail, we remember and we forget.

I need you to do nothing with my suffering other than to love, allowing it and allowing me, without explanation, without your persistent preaching of directions to explore.

Please don't impart your pseudo-spiritual intellectualisation of who and what God is upon what you call the illusion of me, or the details of how that God factually works, objectionably making the case for your heady ideas being the only answers to all questions never asked.

I don't need you to take me away from this human experience.

My share is an invitation for you to join me in it. Come, be intimate with me.

The intimacy of sharing our humanity in the safety of loving acceptance, without the unspoken agenda of wanting me to change, or your judgmental righteousness of only seeing me through the dogma of your adopted ideas.

Let's share joy and explore our ideas of truth, knowing that is all they can be, ideas, without allowing any ideas of non-separation separating us.

Let's embrace our ability to differ, to see with the eyes of our unique experiences of our lives lived, so that living together becomes the natural order of difference, not the undercurrent persistence of conformity to just one understanding.

You and I may be the ocean and the waves, the stars and the dust I've not cleaned off my TV for a week. You and I are in this messy experience of life that so many live trying to understand and then preach to explain.

I don't need you to explain.

Please don't tell me you know who we really are, repeatedly expressing your own egotistic discoveries now entrenched in your own disidentification with the human form. It is there you move away from me, claiming truths that have kept mankind disharmonious for millennia.

If, as you suggest, I cry because in my humanness I've forgotten I'm not human, your cries of dogmatic ideals calling out wrongs only show me a cult refusing to see the kaleidoscope of the beliefs we develop naturally as being human.

And from your egotistic insistence of truth you leave me. You create the separation you claim is an illusion by your insistence on only one belief.

I don't need you to take me away from me, make outrageous claims about what you see that dismiss with justification what it is to be me.

Hello, are you here? Being with me? Without looking to take me anywhere?

Are you being with me?

Are you being?

With me.

# Lighten Up

*'If you lightened up a little you might see something new.'*

Another of those throw-away comments made in a conversation with a client that was later reflected back to me as having the most impact.

In that moment he realised his seriousness was his way of clinging on to knowing. Knowing something to be true, something to be right or wrong, holding white-knuckled on to an opinion he felt as truth. Holding on to the suffering of the illusion of knowing.

In lightening up, he lightened his grip on what he thought he knew, he became light-hearted. The lightness of his heart both lifted him and shined a light for him to see something new.

We cannot see something new whilst we fill our attention with the old. Be that how we think someone should have behaved, how the world should be, or any other expectation and misunderstanding.

To know limits.

When my knowing feels heavy, if my knowing has me feel upset, it's definitely time to 'lighten up.' One of those wonderful expressions with multiple meanings.

Lighten up - let go of the heaviness of knowing.

Lighten up - allow some light in to see beyond the darkness of our current way of seeing.

*'Once I lightened up I saw almost immediately that the situation was nothing at all like I had imagined. You'd probably call it allowing the light of love to shine so we get to see something new with compassionate eyes.'*

Yeah, I might say something like that...

# Following Your Heart

I was asked recently what I might say to a daughter who was considering dating or spending her life with someone 'considerably' older than her. I gave an answer at the time but have been reflecting on it since, because the inquiry strikes at the core of my work with all my clients and is energised by my own experiences and lessons.

My answer is essentially the same for everyone, irrespective of whether the supposed issue is an age difference of ten, twenty or thirty years, or a difference in race, culture, religion, size, shape, colour, cast, class, gender, or any other social construct.

Just follow your heart and be with the person you love and want to be with, irrespective of any cultural or societal norms.

In life I don't believe in painting by numbers. When we do we are bound by predetermined shapes and the picture will always look the same, and is never a true representation of what is in our heart.

George Bernard Shaw summed this up beautifully when he said "The reasonable man adapts himself to the world: the unreasonable one persists in trying to adapt the world to himself. Therefore all progress depends on the unreasonable man."

Go be unreasonable. Love unreasonably. Be ridiculously unreasonable.

Regarding age, none of us knows how long we have on this planet, and whilst it's undeniable our age in years alters the odds, we could as easily be with someone young who passes prematurely than with someone older who lives a very long, happy life. I don't want to live life playing the odds and a numbers game. Someone's energetic age and youthfulness is rarely represented by their age in years.

I have my own experiences around this, and can speak with authenticity about the consequences of not following your heart and instead complying with societal norms. They have been very hard lessons for which I'm grateful and determined not to repeat.

There are numerous couples of different ages, race, religion, etc, that live very happy, fun and loving lives. Because it is the fun and love that keeps them together.

Yet even these arguments entertain the issue intellectually. We cannot resolve matters of the heart with the head. Compliance is the enemy of joy, it stifles progress, and is a distraction from love.

So without rationale, to that daughter, to anyone, I say this:

Please do not allow yourself to be distracted by societal norms that are essentially all from fear.

If you find someone you simply love being with, be with them.

Be with that person with whom you laugh, with whom life is fun, with whom you can share absolutely everything. With whom you can talk about nail paint and the meaning of life. Who adores you and loves your ass off.

Some will say you can love anyone, and there is truth in that, but we are in an energetic dance with each other, and the energy of each connection is unique. We can do a pseudo-spiritual bypass on that, but that just looks inhumane to me.

If, when you're with someone, it feels like nothing else matters, listen to that because nothing else really does matter. Your heart is giving you clues, listen to them.

Listen to your heart. The love that is in your heart. Love will guide you and help you navigate all.

A few years ago speaking to my son about a choice he was considering, not directly related but the principle was the same, I asked him "Do you know what I think?"
Without hesitation, "Yes," he replied, "Do what I want."

Yes. With love.

*It might look like happiness you're chasing,
but really you're chasing misery.*

# Loving Regrets

'No Regrets!'

It's a popular mantra. I've seen people with it inked on their body.

Regret is defined as 'to feel sad, repentant, or disappointed over (something that one has done or failed to do).'

If I've lived life without regrets, without feeling sad or repentant, or disappointed in some way, I've not really lived at all. I've played it safe, I've talked myself out of experiences and suppressed emotions that are all part of being alive.

Without regrets I haven't risked anything that means something to me.

I want to live WITH regrets, rather than avoid them, and to love life and myself all ways and anyways. I want the 'oops' rather than the 'what ifs'. I want the stories to tell my grandchildren, to share the lessons of evolution.

I want the burning of time passed that I would like to have lived differently, because I want to have experimented, taken risks, stepped into choppy waters, emerged from almost drowning.

I want to screw up and wish I hadn't, I want that imagination to expand in me, have my heart burst open without the suppression of any 'no regrets' bullshit.

I'm good with regrets, I'm not looking to avoid them because I don't allow them to eat at me, they teach me, they caress me as I breathe, they remind me how precious this life is and there is nothing to get right or wrong. Sadness, disappointments and regrets come with life, and we have a choice to try and avoid them, resist them, resist life, or simply love them as a part of living a full life.

And it seems to me that as time passes, the things for which I had regrets end up being some of the most beautiful experiences and lessons in life. Out of so many of those experiences I am enriched, I am both softened and resilient, I am compassionate and understanding, I am grateful and am free.

Once I see regret as a natural response to wanting life to go a certain way when it's gone another, and recognise that I am still always taken care of, that life loves me always, and that even my sadness always comes from love, regrets just looks part of a life lived without resistance to its twists, turns and bumps. Without resistance to having my heart broken open so that I may love deeper than ever before.

I don't need to brush off things I wish had gone or done differently in a dismissal of my wants, desires and preferences. I can be kind to myself and my regrets, embrace them as part of my life lived freely. I can be kind by not lying to myself about those wants, preferences and desires. To live a life denying regrets is to live life without sincerity.

I want to live a sincere life, being honest about my preferences, open with my sadness, generous with my sharing of my humanity.

I'm willing to live with regrets tomorrow when I have lived with love and sincerity today.

# Mean Lessons

The relief was palpable.

"You mean things just happen, and there might not be a lesson?"

"There might be something for you to learn from the experience, but that doesn't mean that's why it happened," I suggested.

It's another common mantra - all things happen for a reason, and it's one of the most self-centred ideas I've ever come across. Such a belief has many of us searching for meaning in events and circumstances that simply isn't there, the absence of which seems to cause immense unnecessary searching and suffering.

The whole idea reminds me of one of my favourite memes: "I've been to the centre of the universe, you weren't there."

It looks to me like the universe and all of life is simply unfolding. Things happen. Other things don't. Any belief that something keeps happening in my life to teach me something, and will continue to happen until I learn some lesson the universe or God is determined to teach me, will likely have me searching for something that simply doesn't exist.

And I guarantee all the time you search for something that doesn't exist, you'll never find it.

That's not the same as asking 'What can I learn from this?' There is nearly always something we can learn, should we choose, but the suggestion that the universe is conspiring to teach us something is at best a self-centred egotistic misunderstanding.

Drop some blue ink into some water (event), the water will turn blue (consequence.) Events happen, and with consequences that can lead to other things happening. Without our thinking about them they have no meaning at all, because meaning is not discovered, it is created. Meaning only exists as an idea or concept.

Meaning only exists as thought.

If I believe all things happen for a reason I'm going to suffer in my quest for that reason, until I see that we don't find meaning in things or in events.

Life looks predominantly benevolent to me, we are part of a system that supports us and lifes relentless quest for the continuation of itself (despite our species' irresponsible determination to destroy it... often through some spiritual bypass... oh don't get me started...)

But any suggestion that things happen to deliberately cause us suffering in order to teach us a lesson is an extraordinarily unkind idea that is out of alignment with the benevolent and loving nature of the universe. And that's all it is, an idea about meaning. A kind of meaning that is extremely mean.

Life is unfolding. Shit happens. Any ideas about what it means is down to us, and it doesn't have to mean anything at all.

What if the universe is really not conspiring to teach us lessons, and is simply unfolding? What if there is nothing being taught us and no obligation to learn? What if the only conspiring is that of a universe unfolding in a way to relentlessly support love and life?

That seems like a much more loving and liberating idea to me...

# Friendship

Surely friendship is the most beautiful thing we can experience here. It is something we can have, not just with those we deem to be 'just friends' but it can be the cornerstone of all our relationships, with our family, brothers and sisters, our mums and dads, our lovers, our children.

How blessed to relate as friends first, to have friendship be the ground on which we build all.

When we look deeply at friendship and what it is - the intimate sharing of ourselves and our humanness, our supporting each other as we journey through life, the unspoken 'I see you, I am here for you, I am here with you,' - then perhaps it makes sense that the loss of any such friendship often brings a mourning that we have lost a part of ourselves.

Yet all that was lost was the momentary mirror and the hand that was in ours. What we saw in the mirror is still within us, and our hand is free to hold others. Time to ask 'what was it in that friendship that touched me so deeply?' and to allow ourselves to feel the missing of it, and in that, noticing the part we played in bringing what we now miss into what was.

What was the friendship within us that we allowed to express through us?

The joy of laughter, repartee, clumsiness of candour, tender affection and confessed dreams, all within us, still. Tears not yet shed, heartfelt joy in conversations flowing like predictive text, the silence between words in connections over wires of thousands of miles.

Each moment within us remains within us. Right where that friendship remains too.

On walks I allow the sky to be my friend, the trees I pass each day too. Pigeons dance in front of me on the pavement, assured, no need to flee. A knowing smile to so many friends also out walking each day, with whom I have never spoken.

Yet we share this.

This! All of this!

Just like you, my dear friend, I also feel all that it is to be human, times of joy and despair, deep connection and loneliness, an awareness of the emptiness of my hand. My free hand, always a free hand to hold yours.

I chuckle at the ridiculousness of it all, the illusions of there even being separate hands. How we are in this together, even when we feel apart.

Intertwined.

My dear friend I think of you and smile.

You will always be, for me, a smile.

*Make space for what you want by letting go of what you don't.*

# Noticing Life

I've noticed, repeatedly, that when I'm not putting energy into things I don't want, into things that showed up I didn't even know I didn't want, when I'm not trying to manage other people's opinions of me or my own opinion of life,

when I'm not trying to do something about someone's 'rejection' because of their story of me, ('I don't want what I've made this mean in my life',) and when I'm not putting energy into feeling crap about not even being able to do anything about those perceived rejections, (which are always a redirection,)

when I'm not berating myself for the stupid things I did when I was just a young and naive forty year old know-nothing,

let alone some of the incomprehensible choices I made as a twenty year-old know-it-all,

when I'm not trying to prevent the injury after the bruise has appeared, when I'm not telling myself 'you should be ten pounds lighter by now you fatty!' or 'don't write that, it will be misunderstood,'

when I'm not scrolling back through old messages and scrolling back through my old life, or kicking myself and rolling my eyes for the hours of scrolling, ranting, and fumbling my way through life's shitty times,

when I'm not comparing what I've produced with what I thought I intended and was in plan number four billion and eighty seven for my day, the new month, the rest of this year at least, when I'm not thinking 'yeah probably shouldn't have hit send, or post, or add to cart and complete'

when I'm not putting so much energy into what I think I might have done wrong, or even differently, with all those years, returned smiles, pay checks and miles,

when I'm not sitting predicting more screw-ups or avoiding being some comically-tragic story on the local evening news,

when I'm not putting energy into listening to my critics and really listen to the angels in my life instead,

basically, when I'm not putting energy into anything that does not feel good...

I have so much more energy for simply enjoying my life.

I have so much more energy for those that show me their love, and I am free and full of energy for the expression and expansion of my love.

Beautiful people, friendships, cakes, invites and hugs, through serendipities appear and are made.

Life just is, and it just is love.

And things do indeed work out.

I've noticed when I love, there is love, and I think that's pretty damn cool.

What have you noticed?
How about you?

# Want to Join a Cult of Limitation?

or be free in love...

Have you noticed the messages?

'Not until this happens will this happen.'

Have you noticed the teachers proliferating these very limited perspectives?

Not until everyone sees the world the way I see it will xyz happen, be it climate change, world peace, the end of suffering, the end of difference...

There's an inherent problem with this kind of teaching, and that is us human beings will always entertain different thoughts, many of which we will believe, irrespective of whether they are true or not.

I've been on a call with one such teacher and at what I thought was the conclusion of our call I said "Okay, I think I see what you're talking about. I don't necessarily agree, but I appreciate how it looks to you, thank you.'

That wasn't acceptable to the teacher. 'If you get off the call now you'll just be saying we can agree to disagree, but that's not where it's at for me.'

Set off the sirens! Because not only is this how cult-leaders hook you in, often unintentionally but being dissatisfied with someone having a different opinion to them, (often aggressively), but also because that's EXACTLY where it's at!

Agreeing to disagree.

Human beings will always disagree, and we need to develop cultures in which difference is completely okay, embraced, appreciated, loved. So okay, in fact, that it almost has no relevance. Because when we are not so consumed with our own personal point of view, be it how we think life works, what will bring peace in the Middle East, or who will win the Ryder Cup this year, when we don't give so much credence to those personal opinions and see them for what they are, it seems to me that something else arises and connects us.

No, it's not some awareness of the lack of separate self or oneness or all being of mind, or some other intellectual pseudo-spiritual concept. It is simply a feeling of love. I'm sure you've had loving, trusting, intimate experiences with people who have no awareness at all that people even talk about these things.

Something seems to arise in us that I'm going to call Love.

It's pretty uncomplicated. It doesn't matter to love what colour you are, what religion you practice, whether you believe in non-duality, atheism or a flat earth.

Love seems to me to be the one phenomenon that unites us all. I don't really know what it is. I don't need to know. I just observe what 'it' seems to facilitate or create.

So it looks to me that in love anything is possible, especially the appreciation of differing opinions and the seemingly precarious current position of life on Earth.

AND... I'm OPEN to seeing something else.

I don't necessarily think we can *only* achieve world peace, halt and reverse climate change or anything else only when we all embrace love.

But part of embracing love is embracing the different perspectives of others, including those that don't believe in love. See, we can be sneaky with it, loving people without them even knowing or realising....

World peace is only possible when xyz?

That's a very limiting belief to be portraying, and I get it, being so limited it must come from fear.

Love always tells me anything is possible. Maybe we want to be looking there....

# Imagining Peace

What really is our best chance of peace and harmony?

A chance that will bring about a harmonious world, that will have us take better care of each other, perhaps even reverse climate change.

There are many teaching some form of spiritual understanding, be it non-duality, one-ness without the one, non-separation, often with complex concepts that challenge our deep-routed ways of seeing our existence.

Some suggest for there to be peace we need to do things differently, and help people to understand who they really are.

Yet in the same offerings, sages of old are quoted, and modern mystics suggested as also being pointers to the wisdom of ages.

Most of these teachings have been around for millennia, and whilst some modern day spiritual teachers invite us to look at any separation as an illusion, some of their teachings and ways of handling disagreements are divisive and discriminatory. Ideas, concepts and proclaimed truths presented in ways that make others wrong, evangelic disciples jumping all over discussions suggesting their way is the only way.

That behaviour is, of course, understandable. Whatever the sages and mystics have been trying to show us for thousands of years, it can only be expressed through metaphor and belief. Until we see the nature of beliefs, even the nature of truth, we're inclined to either defend it, or preach it.

What if we consider 'truth' as a concept too?

If we really are to do something different, how about we focus on the simplicity of the human experience? The simplicity of accepting difference?

Instead of offering an alternative belief labelled as truth, what if we simply helped people see the nature of beliefs?

No need to know who you are, what is God, Consciousness, true nature, true essence, your being, or any other idea that is often complex and almost always contrary to popular belief?

What if we didn't need to offer something else for us to argue over and debate? Nothing to preach, teach, convince, inquire or deride. Just an understanding that however we see anything, be it the world, spirituality, God, who we are, we are making it all up.

What if instead of trying to teach people a truth, we helped people see how we construct what we believe to be truth?

Imagine if we're no longer trying to have people think the same as us about the world, spirituality, God, who we are, but helping them to see that it's completely okay to see all of those differently.

Because we can't not see them differently.

What might happen if we realised we didn't need others to think the same as us?

What might happen if people saw the fallacy of their own thinking? What might arise from really seeing that it's okay to see and be different?

What might arise from that? Perhaps a phenomenon we might call love.

Once we see the nature of beliefs, could it be that peace would be possible irrespective of our beliefs?

You see, in the same way as I don't care how big your genitals are, I really don't care what you believe, provided you're not trying to ram it down my throat.

It seems to me that by nature we're all curious how each sees the world, and when we understand that however that is, that it can only ever be imagined, it doesn't have to mean anything, and we can be together in the joy of the exploration of our differences. Embracing them as gifts.

I can even love that you seem separate from me, and want to be with you anyway.

There really are no conditions to peace, only those we create, including perhaps inadvertently any teachings that suggest we must understand who we are for there to be peace.

We do not need to see anything the same.

Peace is available. It's free. The free Peace.

"You may say I'm a dreamer, but I'm not the only one."

Imagine…

# Moonlight

'Hey do you see the moon?'

The water laps around my ankles, I notice the swirls of it, it wrapping and finding its way around my legs, around me.

'It's so beautiful! So peaceful! You have to see it! Come, take a look at the moon.'

Lapping away, it's relentless, alive, wave after wave, some more gentle than others.

'You can't truly love unless you understand the moon.'

Each wave ebbs away and I feel the sand move beneath my feet, as I sink a little into the ground.

'Hey, dreamer, sleeper... take a look at the moon.'

I watch a single wave arrive, then recede, overlapped by another. They are eternal, life's relentlessness for itself.

'Do you even know yourself? Come on! Look at this moon!'

It's all so incredibly blue. When do ripples become waves? Do they have their own little graduation ceremonies before they embark on their final journey to the shore?

'Pssst! Wakey wakey! Peace is only possible this way, take a look at the moon.'

I move my half-buried feet and turn towards the shore, the warm sands caressing my toes as a gull lifts into the sky.

'It's all an illusion, buddy, come on, take a look at the moon.'

A few steps, a knowing nod shared with a fellow wanderer, white houses and red roofs inland invite my attention.

'Hey seeker, happiness is not there. Let me show you who you are. Take a look at the moon.'

A few hundred yards ahead I see a small wooden structure in the sand, protecting a turtles nest. As the sun goes down and the sky ambers, I imagine the miracle of baby turtles scuttling into the blue Ionian sea.

'Hey, it's vital you ask yourself who am I? Come on, take a look at the moon.'

Further in the distance a couple walk hand-in-hand, headed into the town. Later they will dance as only two intimately known bodies can.

'Let me show you truth, come on, take a look at the moon!.'

The air is cool now, my skin calls my attention as I stand to look around. My final evening here, for now.

'Hey you who thinks you're a body! Come on, don't look there, it's not helpful. Come on, dude, come look at the moon.'

I breathe in the moment, a single moment of beauty in this life, on the beach, on my favourite island. Sometimes I come here and feel lost, and sometimes I come here, found. A million emotions among the grains of sand.

Yeah, here, this place, this life, this moment, I am home. Always home.

There's a glisten on the ocean.

Glancing up I notice the moon.

*We evolve, often beyond the ideas people in our lives have of us. Allow the evolution. Allow yourself.*

No longer trying to change has been the biggest change for
me
An ending that has brought about so many new beginnings
The end of the quest for answers has dissolved so many
questions
No longer searching to find freedom I am free
To simply dance with life
And enjoy being me

# Clearing Space to Not Know

In the last seven days I have unsubscribed from 28 email lists, and deleted a similar number of email folders where I was just storing each email without reading them. Some of these are email lists of dear friends, I wonder if they have noticed...

Even digitally, creating space by clearing out stuff that is not of genuine interest to us makes it so much easier to see what is.

And instead of FOMO (fear of missing out), there's actually a JOMO (joy of missing out) which I'm bringing to other areas of my life.

I've noticed I save so much time and energy when I don't engage in some of the endless discussions and intellectual pseudo-spiritual sparring on social media about who or what is God, often disguised as spiritual teachings and wisdom.

These discussions and questions may look like fun, and indeed maybe they really are for some, but whenever I explore with people where we're asking from, the searching for answers almost always comes from a place of insecurity and fear, an endless quest to know who we are, the significance of which is proliferated by well-meaning teachers offering replacement beliefs presented as truths to satisfy that perceived need to know.

Facebook reminds me of my own previous teachings in its 'memories' feature, and I'm amused as I, too, thought I was offering truths to replace unhelpful beliefs.

Now it just looks like there is only belief, only concepts, only ways through which we can see and navigate this world, and I've explored so many of them over the last twenty two years, including the currently increasingly popular non-duality.

In seeing the nature of beliefs and that which we think we know of as 'true' it no longer makes sense to search through the plethora of answers that were arriving in my inbox every day. It no longer makes sense to explore more content.

Once we see we really don't need to know, (and perhaps can never really know,) the searching naturally comes to an end.

And here we are.

Here.
Now.
Present.

Not knowing and being okay with that.

And suddenly I notice in the space what was being obscured by the search...

A life.

Navigated by lots of meanings that don't need to mean anything. I could call that freedom, but there's meaning in that too.

In so much space it's even more obvious when the perceived need to know pops up, and I chuckle, amused at the attempts to be hoodwinked away from now.

In being okay with missing out and no longer searching to know I realise I'm not missing out at all.

There's such joy in that.

The joy of not knowing

# Goodbye Waves to Everything

Not so long ago my biggest blind spot was making claims
of seeing and that I know
I was relentless, so clear. You had to hear.

Some examples - the small matter of what God is,
And who we are, or how love and what some call
'consciousness' actually work.
I could answer that quiz.

And the more I looked through the lens of knowing, the
more it looked like I knew.

I had discovered a truth after my decades of searching,
my ego's quest for an egoless existence
was suitably encouraged, fooled and subdued.

The world looked the way it did because I was looking at
it that way.

Blind in my illusion of knowing, I couldn't even see
that I couldn't even see.

I'd even published two books believing I knew, musings
indeed.

Until, in one conversation, in particular one throwaway remark,
the illusion of knowing fell away.
Stark!

Dissolved.

That was over two years ago, and I hid away for a while.
Everything I had been pointing towards and teaching for years,
things that I would have argued wholeheartedly as true,
I was seeing for the first time as built on sand.

Standing on shifting lands.

Initially it was disorientating, to suddenly navigate a life of not knowing. Let's face it, even the most spiritual teachings,
by definition, point to something, being known.

In a single moment the tide had come in and washed everything away.

Yet, once the disorientation passed, in the not knowing I've experienced a beautiful freedom.

Others have noticed it in me too.

No longer a meanness in meaning-making.
Much laughter follows through.

No longer confined by limitations of knowing.
Boundless love and infinite possibilities now the dance.

No more faithless projections of my way of seeing out
into a 'if only you got this' world.
I'm getting a new world with every glance.

No longer trying to teach the world how the world works.
Peace over preach ensues.

So to now, perhaps enlightened by my blindness,
here I am, observing, often in utter amusement,
the knowing, explaining and meaning-making
deemed necessary to navigate a world
predicated on the insecure based misunderstanding
that we need to know.

Theorems, concepts and proclamations abound.
All made of sand.

And I chuckle at how real that looks,
sometimes in awe at the elaborate nature and elaborate
shapes
of so many sandcastles along the shore.
Blessed with such joy and freedom in not knowing anymore.

And so the tide flows.

Bravo, life, bravo!

*If you say you don't want strawberries, and you keep eating strawberries, you want strawberries.*

# A Change from Four Years in Four Seconds

It was fascinating to see as particular post appear in my Facebook memories feed from four years ago. If you had a conversation with me then, or in the preceding twelve years and a couple of years after, I would have been pointing you to what seemed true for me - that all separation is an illusion and the only truth is Love.

I was all-in on these 'truths', on these ways of seeing our existence, our essence, who we are, God. My own venture into the 'paradigm often taught as truth' of non-duality was mostly a quiet one, certainly not one of criticising and kicking up a fuss. That, to me, just seems somewhat contradictory and hypocritical. But I would watch and observe all the teachers that were bleating out concepts around managing our thoughts and experiences, reinforcing illusions of separation or various dependencies on love, and often silently exclaim with a degree of egotistic frustration - 'You just don't get it!'

Then, late in 2017, in a conversation someone said just nine words to me, which probably took no longer than four seconds to say, that set off a grenade among what looked like truth to me. It was one of those 'What the???" moments that washed away the sandcastles of what I'd been pointing people towards for well over a decade.

As the tide of change ebbed away, and I crawled out of the cave I'd used to sit and settle, I started to see that it wasn't realising that what I had been teaching were sandcastles that had disorientated me, but that everything is.

At best, we get a sense of some concept of truth from what I'll simply describe as the formless infinity, and define it as some kind of sandcastle in this world of form. Even knowing it is only a representation, there we are attempting to represent that which simply cannot ever be. You cannot represent the formless in form.

Woah, a little divergence into pseudo-spiritual speak...

To put this another way, in those four seconds and the waves of unravelling that appeared after, it wasn't more content or more truth, a better truth or a single truth that appeared. It was an unveiling of the nature of beliefs and the nature *of* truth, and a realisation of how it is our quest for truth and relentless searching that so often has us suffer. It is and has always been the preaching of single truths, single paradigms, single beliefs packaged as truth, the instilling of ways of living and looking at the world, that have brought about so many wars, divided us and kept us from peace.

If I talk with a such a teacher there will be things they see that I don't, and that I see that they don't. The big difference between us will be that they will believe my not seeing what they see keeps me and the world from peace, and I need to 'get it', whereas it looks to me my embracing that we see things so differently, without any resistance to that, actually allows peace.

Peace exists and awaits among our differences.

Now, I see teachers sharing what I was doing two years ago, four years ago, ten years ago, with such strength of conviction they will willingly lose friends, criticise, even insult, in the name of a single truth that will solve all the problems that keep us from love & peace.

And I once again catch myself, this time chuckling greatly at my own egotistic judgment of 'you just don't get it!' Such is the paradox of believing one sees the nature of belief. Yet I am oh so open to seeing something new, something as yet unknown, something that completely contradicts how it all looks to me.

I'm open to any belief I have today becoming myth tomorrow, whilst also seeing the nature of truth and beliefs, I don't even need them to change to be free from them.

Seeing their nature I no longer need to seek or inquire and attempt to be free of them. I can be completely at peace with different beliefs and truths to you, whoever you are, irrespective of any understanding or if you really are not separate from me.

It all becomes sooooo irrelevant.

And I also notice that, when I'm with someone, or within any community, without teaching of opinion, belief or truth, if we allow the teachings to subside, allow our thoughts about our differences to subside, we're able to be with each other in a harmony that cannot be described in words that really can only ever separate through their definition.

Our sharing of our differences can even become a joyous activity of togetherness.

Maybe it really is the teaching of truths and beliefs that keeps us at war, and keeps us from what seems to arise in the absence of any 'you need to see this, or else you just don't get it' kind of thinking.

Maybe it is Love that arises in that space of indifference about our differences.

At least that's my favourite idea, my favourite belief, my favourite truth.

I think that's worth four seconds of anyone's time

# I Fall in Love With My Clients

As we sat together on our call my heart swelled, and I was reminded in that moment just how beautiful it is to be with someone in this way.

Present, in full acceptance, filled with gratitude for simply being with each other in this moment.

Such moments don't really take us places, even if we are reminiscing with someone or making plans. These moments of love and connection serve to remind us of what is here.

Hello, Love

That term, 'fall in love', is so often used to describe the objectification of love. It creates a dependency for love, and often one that, eventually, can never be met. It's often laced with ideas of romance and attraction.

Yet to truly be in love with someone is to be in the energy of love, in their presence, without ideas. To meet each other in the energy of love, without objectification, without agenda or destination, without any conditions at all. The pure, uncontaminated space and presence of love.

What's the significance of this when coaching?

Just consider for a moment how it feels to be in the energy of love. How does it feel to know you are loved, unconditionally, without judgment or agenda? When I ask this question most people answer with some adjective such a beautiful, but also free. Free to simply be, to explore, to express and say whatever comes to mind. Free to challenge, yet also be undefended, to experiment, to play.

And this for me is the essence of coaching; to be present, to be exploring without boundaries to possibility, in full allowance of whatever it is to be human.

My clients and I will often express love for each other on our calls, and yet our declarations are not really about each other. They are simply an expression of our being in the energy of love. We're feeling love in that moment, the other person just happens to be with us there too.

Of course there's much more to coaching and mentoring than simply sitting with someone in a space of love, trust and care.

But it's a beautiful foundation for a coaching.

It's a beautiful foundation for everything.

# A Spiritual Paradox

Perhaps the most unspiritual thing you can do is call out the behaviour of others as non-spiritual.

Perhaps the most unspiritual thing you can do is criticise, after all, aren't we are all expressions of the divine, even when we think we are not?

Perhaps the most unspiritual thing you can do is dismiss the personal or the self.

Perhaps the most unspiritual thing you can do is compare and suggest there is right and wrong, or there are such things as mistakes.

Perhaps the most unspiritual thing you can do is to teach, to preach, your beliefs, that you claim are not beliefs but true.

Perhaps the most unspiritual thing you can do is to lay claim to an understanding of God, consciousness or spirit.

Perhaps the most unspiritual thing you can do is to make claims of spiritual knowing, or indeed any knowing at all.

Perhaps the most unspiritual thing you can do is to suggest it's even possible to be unspiritual.

Perhaps there is no such thing as unspiritual at all...

# Being All-in

Being 100% committed to something is oh so much easier than just 98 or 99%

When you're all-in, 100% committed, a decision or choice has been made. Whatever shows up is dealt with in the context of that decision having been taken. Whatever shows up is dealt with in the context of 'what is.'

Being only 98% or 99% committed, however, leaves room for deliberation, rumination, and constant reconsidering a decision. Basically more thinking.

This is not the same as simply not knowing. That's a different game. Not knowing is totally cool, and in a similar vein I suggest dropping all rumination or trying to work things out. Allow the space to move from unknown to known. It will happen without you.

But for most of us, we have situations in our lives, in our businesses and in our relationships where we are almost all-in, just not quite. We kind of know, but keep that 1 or 2% back.

Because we're scared...

It might look scary being 'all-in' yet really life is so much easier that way. Of course, things show up that have us change course, have us reconsider and change direction. But if your default is to always look at the gap in commitment, the getting out, the questioning of a decision, your life will be much more of a mind-mess than if you're simply all-in.

This is how I have made some major changes in my life. Losing weight, moving, changing jobs, building a business. This is also why in coaching I offer no refunds and ask that clients pay upfront. We remove the half-assed-ness so we're all-in to making it work. We're committed to our time together and get on with making the most of that, whatever shows up.

In relationships this all-in basically means when something shows up you deal with it in the context of allowing the relationship to work. That's the default, finding a way to build trust, intimacy and understanding. When things show up they become opportunities to get to know each other and connect more deeply.

When you're all-in, anything that shows up becomes an invitation to look for a way deeper in, rather than a way out.

When you're only 98% or 99% in, such opportunities become a feeder for doubt, rumination, berating and fear. Always a step away from your heart and into your head.

Want an easy life? Go all-in.

Then show up and deal with what shows up.
100%
With love.

You'll be okay.
Life will love you back

# Dreaming With The Light On

In February last year I experienced a bout of depression like I hadn't experienced in years. I noticed some occasional self-judgment about it; here I am, a professional coach of fifteen years, yet I was on a right old downer about life. Let's face it, feeling depressed sucks! It feels like it sucks the life out of you, and sucks away who you are...

If you're in similar communities to me on social media or follow some of the same people, you probably also get to see the suggestion that the only thing we need to know is who we really are. Knowing who you are is the direct path to harmony, relinquishing of suffering, world peace... Then there are the claims of no claims. Once you know you know, and all else becomes irrelevant.

I used to believe this too, subscribing to it as a truth, after all it's a mantra preached by even the most spiritually respected teachers and gurus. 'Be still and know you are God.'

Yet in the same way I was looking for a way out of my depression, to escape where I was not, looking to know who you are is an impossible quest and can only ever be limiting.

To know limits.

Our freedom is in not knowing, as much as we chase and seek to know. Our freedom is in the undefined.

It looks to me that there is freedom in simply seeing who and what we are not. The moment we look to define who and what we are, we confine ourselves into more concepts and ideas.

'God is a concept by which we measure our pain.' - A beautiful line from the song, God, by John Lennon and Plastic Ono Band. Check it out.

Noticing what and who we are not frees us from those concepts and ideas. Seeing we are not any of the ideas we have about ourselves. It was seeing this again earlier last year that reminded me I could be free from the experience of depression. I can remember the exact moment, sitting at my mother's house, her inquiring how I was feeling and my reminding her that really it wasn't helpful to keep talking about it and putting energy there. Then I noticed... wow... I had started to identify with this guy, 'Phil who is depressed.'

What the?...

I knew deep down I was not that guy, so that moment of noticing the identification creeping into my way of being was like a light being turned on. Suddenly I was awake to who I was not.

I was experiencing intense feelings that we describe as depression, yet I knew that was not who I am. I am not my experience. Ever.

I didn't do anything with this noticing. Once the light was on I didn't need to do anything more to be able to see. And when I returned to my mother's a few days later we both noticed I was no longer feeling depressed. It had passed, just as any feeling can and will. Would it have done so had I not noticed? Yes, for sure, but in my experience likely after much more time, simply because the concept of identifying with a feeling, like any diagnosis, reinforces it. The subtle yet profound difference between 'I am depressed' and 'I am experiencing feelings of depression.' The difference between 'I am injured' and 'there is a cut on my left hand.'

For those feelings of depression to dissolve I did not need to know who I truly am, that I am God, to remember my true essence or true nature, that we are all one and not separate. I didn't need to know anything. I simply noticed who I was not. I was not and am not any feeling I experience.

All identity is a dream, including any ideas and concepts of who you really are. Letting go of all those ideas and concepts, all those beliefs, or at least noticing that they are at play, noticing that we are dreaming, has been the most liberating thing for me, and many of my clients.

What's beyond those ideas, concepts and beliefs? We cannot ever really know. We might feel we get glimpses, but then comes interpretation which is always a function of the intellect. To know we must interpret and create meaning. We must create a dream.

At the end of the song, Lennon says 'The dream is over.' Seems to me he's incorrect. The nightmare may be over, but the dream continues, only with awareness that it is a dream. Kind of dreaming with the light on.

And when I know I'm dreaming it seems to matter so much less what's going on. Happy or sad, cheerful or depressed. I often chuckle when I catch myself thinking I know who I am, much as I do at those preaching their dream too.

Once I remembered I was not 'Phil who is depressed' it didn't matter so much how I felt. I knew I wasn't that, it was just going on.

Other versions of this dream continue to show up, like 'I am in love' or 'I am lonely.' It's fascinating to watch the determination to establish an identity, to define. To know and understand.

Who am I? I have plenty of ideas and have no chuffing clue.

But I do like to dream.
And I do like ice cream.

Do we really need to make anything else matter?...

*Smile. The rest will sort itself out.*

# You Say You Want Love and Peace

Yet put all your focus and attention on people and things,
Circumstances, concepts and ceremony rings.
On people pleasing, or not, freedom from and being with
people, friendships or fiends,
Cards, stars, energy circles, unicorns, crystals, signs and
calendar dates,
The poets, gurus and other greats
Teachers, ideas, searches and finds
Hallucinogenic induced states of mind,
Always juggling another idea,
Always only ever based on fear,
Of missing an opportunity to finally be free,
To ascend, transcend, an egoless version of an idea of 'me'
Another concept, new principles, something else to explore,
Another reason to renounce now and deplore
Always getting ready, preparing and avoiding, pushing and
pulling, chained, never free
Unlovingly searching for peace
Turning still waters into choppy seas

You say you want love yet reject everything that is,
You've been searching for answers for so many years

If you want peace, take a direct look
Beyond all concepts and objects
You'll see where it's at
If you want love, just let love in.
Without all of that tat.

Love and peace are free.
You need not try.
It's only your chasing objects, concepts and ideas
That needs to die.

Love always, love all ways

# I'd Love to Help You

To have what you want.

Especially if that's to experience more love and joy.

And especially if that's feel more connected.

To your spouse or partner.
To your children, parents or siblings.
To your friends or colleagues.
To your clients.

But most of all, I'd love to help you feel more connected to you and your life.

When I reflect back on all the coaching I've been doing since 2005, it's almost exclusively around relationships, business and personal, and those relationships always have a foundation in our relationship with ourselves.

For me to change my relationships with abusive partners, I've had to change my relationship with me, who I thought I was, who I am, to really see me and allow myself to love me and be loved. Warts and all. To see through my perceived imperfections and see the amazing man I am, to allow myself to know what I bring to intimate relationships, irrespective of any insecure stories that appear. I've experienced some of the most beautiful and intimate connections in this respect, been loved how I wish to be loved, and out of romantic relationships have even developed beautiful friendships of honesty and trust that are now immensely treasured.

For my relationship with my Dad, who disowned me for ten years, for that relationship to change, I had to change my relationship with me, my relationship with my judgment, my relationship with my stories of my Dad. In the dissolution of those stories I have seen him for the first time, for who he really is, his struggles and his stories, and after over forty years on this planet actually fully allowed myself to feel love for him. What a beautiful gift that has been for me, as well as for him.

For my relationships with my colleagues to change I needed to change my relationship with the guy I saw as me in the workplace, from a misfit to someone who was loved as a leader, I needed to change my relationship with my stories of limitation so that I could allow myself to progress to some very senior positions with strong salaries, and then also allow myself to follow my dream to be completely free of corporate life, to help others live their most joyous life of love and connection. To help others feel free.

To change my relationships with my friends I've had to change my relationship with the guy who held on and borderline begged people to spend time with him, to change my relationship with the friend I thought I was so that I could allow myself to be in friendships that both of us want, to let love in, to allow friendships to be easy, fruitful, prosperous and loving. Letting go of long-term friendships has been the most painful thing I've had to do this past couple of years, yet it has also been the most liberating. Once again I've learned to love the friend that is me.

And to change the relationship with my clients, I've had to change my relationship with my business, which in turn has required me to change my relationship with me and the part I play in that business. From being a needy, creepy, client-seeking geeky, from spammy hellos to nurtured connections and genuine relationships with people. I've allowed my own love, curiosity and interest in people, the utter awesomeness that is people, to guide me and connect me to wonderful clients with whom conversations are a blast. Such fun, and soooo much love.

And to allow myself to fully enjoy life, I've had to change my relationship with my perception of life, with how I think it should be, to shift from a desperate desire to control and know, to simply allowing myself to be immersed in all of it, so freely, some might say recklessly, yet actually so matter-of-factly that even the most significant changes in my life don't phase me at all. It just is. Loving life just is...

Of course it's not all giggles and friendgasms.

There are times of anxiousness, sadness, even heartbreak. But my relationship with those experiences has changed too, such that they no longer seem like experiences to be avoided. Such amazing freedom in that, allowing myself to be fully in my life, connected to me and everyone and everything in it.

Allowing myself to love.

So I'd love to help you too!

How would you love to be more connected?
To your spouse, partner, lover?
To your children?
To your business?
To you?

To love?

I'd love to help you come to know your freedom to allow yourself to be immersed in this beautiful life, free from endless spiritual searching or goal-chasing. Free from being a constant self-improvement project.

I'd love to help you and talk with you.
How about you?

*The questions and doubts never stop, I am just more aware of them and who is asking; and in that, I see their irrelevance.*

# About the Author

Phil Goddard helps people create easy, prosperous and loving personal & professional relationships. He is an internationally renowned life & relationship coach, speaker, leadership consultant, and lover of life and humanity. The author of *Musings on Love* and *More Musings on Love*, he is also the host of both The Coaching Life and Naked Hearts Podcasts. His work centres around transforming relationships and leadership through developing a deeply grounded understanding of the principles behind our human experience and the nature of how our experience of life is created.

With humour and sincerity, he combines over twenty-one years in corporate leadership with fifteen years as a professional coach, to help organisations build harmonious and highly productive teams, and individuals to live their most loving and joyous lives.

He has coached Hollywood actors, international models, journalists, artists, authors, film directors, corporate executives, and numerous business owners, leaders and entrepreneurs.

He challenges his work on happiness by following a few English sports teams.

He is a digital nomad living between Asia and Europe, and can often be found on the Greek Island of Zakynthos, where he holds exclusive coaching immersion retreats for individual clients.

Phil can be contacted via philg.com and found on Facebook via fbphil.com

Printed in Great Britain
by Amazon

74361559R00122